BRITTANY & ITS BYWAYS:

SOME ACCOUNT OF

ITS INHABITANTS AND ITS ANTIQUITIES;

DURING A RESIDENCE IN THAT COUNTRY.

BY MRS. BURY PALLISER.

WITH NUMEROUS ILLUSTRATIONS.

LONDON:
JOHN MURRAY, ALBEMARLE STREET.
1869.

The right of Translation is reserved.

LK 2482

BRITTANY & ITS BYWAYS:

SOME ACCOUNT OF

ITS INHABITANTS AND ITS ANTIQUITIES;

DURING A RESIDENCE IN THAT COUNTRY.

BY MRS. BURY PALLISER.

WITH NUMEROUS ILLUSTRATIONS.

LONDON:
JOHN MURRAY, ALBEMARLE STREET.
1869.

The right of Translation is reserved.

PRINTED BY WILLIAM CLOWES AND SONS, DUKE STREET, STAMFORD STREET,
AND CHARING CROSS.

CONTENTS.

CHERBOURG—Mont du Roule—Visit of Queen Victoria—Harbour, 1—Breakwater—Dock-Yard, 2—Chantereyne—Hôpital de la Marine, 3—Castle—Statue of Napoleon I.—Library—Church of La Trinité, 4—Environs—Octeville, 5—Lace-school of the Sœurs de la Providence, 11.

QUERQUEVILLE—Church of St. Germain, 5—Château of the Comte de Tocqueville, 6.

TOURLAVILLE—Château, 7—Crêpes, 11.

MARTINVAST—Château, 12.

BRICQUEBEC—Castle—History, 12—VALOGNES, 14.

ST. SAUVEUR-LE-VICOMTE—Demesne—History, 15—Castle—Convent—Abbey, 16.

PÉRIERS, 17—La Haye-du-Puits, 17—Abbey of Lessay—Mode of Washing—Inn-signs, 18—Church, 19.

COUTANCES—Cathedral—Churches, 19—Fête of St. Fiacre, 20.

GRANVILLE—Situation—History—Church, 21—View from the "Roc"—Bathing-machines—Defeat of the Vendean army—Death of La Rochejacquelin, 22—Costume of the Women—Environs—St. Pair, 23.

AVRANCHES—Extensive View—Scene of Absolution of Henry II.—Cemetery, 24.

PONTORSON—Story of the Lady Typhaine, 24—Government by Du Guesclin—Mont St. Michel, 25—Chapel of St. Aubert—Visits of English kings—Pilgrimages of Kings of France, 26—Convent of "La Merveille," 27—Isle of La Tombeleine—Prison, 28—The Iron Cage, 29.

DOL-DE-BRETAGNE—Street Architecture, 30—Cathedral, 31—Tomb of Bishop James—Chapel of St. Samson, 32—Monks, 33—Dyke, 34—Menhir, 35—Château of Combourg, 36—Chateaubriand, 37.

CANCALE — Oysters, 37 — Wretched public vehicles, 38 — Bay, 39.

ST. MALO — Situation, 39 — Sea-wall, 40 — Tomb of Chateaubriand — Memorials of him, 41 — Watch-dogs, 42 — Castle — History, 43 — DINARD, 44.

DINAN — Ascent of the Rance — Statue of Du Guesclin, 44 — Siege of 1359 — Duel of Du Guesclin and Thomas of Cantorbéry, 45 — Castle of Montfilant — Story of Gilles de Bretagne, 46 — Lunatic Asylum — Castle of Dinan, 50 — Church of St. Sauveur, 51 — Museum, 52 — Environs — Château of La Bellière, 54 — Chateau of La Garaye — Count Claude de la Garaye and his Wife, 57 — Jugon, 61 — Castle of La Hunaudaye, 62 — Legend of La Hunaudaye, 63 — Forest of La Hunaudaye — The Chouan War, 66.

LAMBALLE — Jeanne la Boiteuse — War of Succession, 67 — Temple of Lanleff, 68 — Tradition of the blood-spots, 70.

ST. BRIEUC — Palais de Justice — Tour de Cesson, 71 — Church of Notre Dame — Review of his army by James II. of England, 72.

GUINGAMP — Situation — Fishing in the Trieux — Sanctuary of Notre Dame du Bon Secours — "Frérie blanche," 72 — Fountain of Duke Peter — Women of Guingamp — Knitting and spinning — Ransom for Du Guesclin, 74 — Chapel of St. Léonard patron saint of prisoners — Curious charms against fever, 75.

PAIMPOL — Château de Boisgelin, 75 — Abbey of Beauport, 76 — Situation of Paimpol — Suspension-bridge of Lézardrieux, 80 — Château of La Roche Jagu, 81.

PONTRIEUX — Castle of La Roche Derrien, 82 — "War of the two Jeannes" — Church of Langoat — Monument of Ste. Pompée, 83 — Burial customs — Excellence of roads in Brittany, 84.

KERMARTIN — St. Ives, 84 — Inscription at his birthplace — Interior of a Breton dwelling, 86 — Church of Minihy-Tréguier — Will of St. Ives, 87.

TREGUIER — Cathedral — Burial-place of St. Ives, 88 — Constable Clisson, 89 — Cemetery, 90 — Skull-boxes, 91.

LANNION — Difficulty of the road, 91 — Perros Guirec — Ploumanach — Roche Pendue, 92 — Situation of Lannion — Fishery — Sea-weed gathering, 94 — Castle of Touquédec, 95 — Château of Kergrist, 96.

MORLAIX — Situation — Timbered houses, 97 — History, 98 — Breton characteristics, 99 — Protestant Missions, 100 — "Fontaine des Anglais," 102 — River Scenery, 103.

ST. POL DE LÉON, 103 — Religious Monuments — Character of the Léonnais, 104 — Church of Notre Dame de Creizker — Legend of St. Génévroc, 105 — Cathedral, 106 — St. Pol and the Dragon, 109 — Ursuline Convent — "Droit de Motte," 110.

ROSCOFF — Contraband trade with England — Vegetable produce, 111 — Historic importance, 112 — Church — Island of Batz — Enormous old fig-tree, 113.

ST. THÉGONNEC STATION — Cabaret — Church, 114 — Guimiliau Church — Sculptures, 115 — Calvary, 116 — Buckwheat, 117 — Castle and Church of La Roche Maurice, 118.

BREST — Situation, 118 — Harbour, 119 — Church of the Folgoët — Legend, 120 — Kersanton stone, 122 — Sculptures in Kersanton stone, 123 — The Fool's Well, 124 — Exterior of Church, 125 — Churchyard, 127 — Monthly Fair of Brest — Peasants' Costumes, 133.

FINISTÈRE — Abbey of St. Mathieu, 129 — Sea-fights, 130 — Pont Launay and Châteaulin, 134.

QUIMPER, 135 — Legend of St. Corentin, 137 — Cathedral, 139 — National costume, 140.

CONCARNEAU, 142 — Sardine Fishery, 143 — Aquarium, 147 — Dolmen and Rocking-stone of Trégunc — Château of Rustéphan, 149 — Valley of Pontaven, 150.

QUIMPERLÉ — Fishing, 151 — Buildings — Tomb of St. Gurloës, 152 — Tomb of John de Montfort — Ruins of St. Columban, 153 — Dirtiness of the Bretons — Animals and Farm produce — Butter Indulgence, 154.

LORIENT — Bisson and the Pirates, 155.

HENNEBONT — Heroic defence by Jeanne de Flandre, 156 — Church of Notre Dame-de-Paradis, 157.

STE. ANNE D'AURAY, 158 — Scala Sancta — Fête, 159 — Chartreuse, 160 — Battle, 161 — Deaf and Dumb School, 164 — Massacre of Quiberon, 165 — Champ des Martyrs, 168 — Celtic Remains, 169.

LOCMARIAKER — Tumulus — Celtic and other Remains, 170 — Tumulus of Gavr' Inis, 175.

CARNAC — Celtic Remains — Menhirs of Kermario, 177 — Legend of St. Cornély, 178 — Jade Celts, &c., at Plouharnel, 180 — Dolmen of Concorro, 181.

VANNES — History — Promenade, 183 — Cathedral, 184 — Château Gaillau — Tour du Connétable, 185 — Model Village of Korner-hoët, 187 — Peninsula of Rhuys, 188 — Fortress of Sucinio, 189 — Abbey of St. Gildas, 192 — Abelard and the Breton Monks, 193 — The Breton "Blue Beard," 194 — Butte d'Arzon — Castle of Elven, 199 — Growth of Chestnuts, 203.

PLOËRMEL, 203 — Church, 204 — Tombs, 205 — Column of the Thirty, 206 — Battle of the Thirty, 207 — Château of Josselin, 209 — Church of Josselin, 213.

MONTFORT-SUR-MER — Forest of Paimpont — Fairy tales, 215.

RENNES, ancient capital of Brittany — Entry of Henry IV. — Scenery of the Loire, 216 — Castle of Champtoceaux, 218.

NANTES — Cathedral, 221 — Tombs, 222 — Castle — Anne of Brittany, 223 — Promenades and Boulevards — Museum, 227 — Jardin des Plantes — Descent of the Loire — The Noyades, 228.

ST. NAZAIRE — Historical associations, 230 — Le Croisic, 232 — Salt-pans, 233 — Costume of the Paludiers, 234 — Saulniers — Chouan: origin of the name and of the War, 241 — Church of Batz, 243 — Situation of Le Croisic, 244 — Chapel of St. Goustan, 245.

GUÉRANDE — Church of St. Aubin — Chapel of Notre Dame Blanche, 246 — La Roche Bernard, 247 — Wedding Festivities, 248 — National Music — Female Costume — Fête de la Vierge and of the Emperor, 249 — Scenery of the River Loch, 250.

BELLE ISLE — Le Palais — M. Trochu's Model Farm, 251 — Breton fatalism, 252 — Grotte du Port Coton, 255 — Historical associations of Belle Isle, 256 — Fishery, 257.

PONT L'ABBÉ, 257 — Costumes, 258 — Church, 259.

LOCTUDY — Romanesque Church, 261.

TORCHE DE PENMARCH, 262 — Church of St. Guenolé, 263 — "Le filet saint" — Ruins of the old Town, 264 — Fontenelle the Leaguer, 267 — Church of St. Nonna, 268 — Menhirs at Kerscaven, 269.

AUDIERNE — Lighthouse — Bathing-machines, 269 — Town, 270.

POINTE DU RAZ — Popular superstitions — Church of St. Collédoc, 271 — "Enfer de Plogoff" — Island of Sein — Druidesses, 272 — Dangerous passage, 273 — Baie des Trépassés — Submerged city of Is, 274 — Legend of King Gradlon and his daughter Dahut, 275.

DOUARNENEZ — Romanesque Church of Pointcroix, 276 — Chapel of Notre Dame de Comfort — Wheel of Sacring-Bells — Town of Douarnenez, 279 — Pardon of Ste. Anne-de-la-Palue, 280 — Costume, 281 — Church of Ste. Anne — Procession, 282 — Holy Well of Ste. Anne, 285.

SCAËR — Old Customs and Superstitions, 285 — Wrestling — "Pierres de Croix," 286.

LE FAOUÉT — Chapel of St. Barbe, 287 — Wedding ceremonies and amusements, 288 — Fishing, 289 — Old Breton superstitious still prevalent — Lavandières de la Nuit, 290 — Church of St. Fiacre — Elaborately carved Rood-screen, 293 — Painted glass — Ruined Castle of Poncallec — Plot of Cellamare, 294 — Montagnes Noires, 296.

CARHAIX — Situation, 297 — Statue of La Tour d'Auvergne, 298 — Fair and Market — Church of St. Tremeur — Skull-boxes, 299.

HUELGOAT, 300 — Lead-mines, 301 — Cascade of St. Herbot — Chapel of St. Herbot, 303 — His tomb, 304 — Patron of cattle — Offerings of horsehair and cows' tails, 304 — Homeward journey, 307.

	PAGE
USEFUL DATES in the History of Brittany	309
CHRONOLOGICAL TABLE of the Dukes of Brittany	310

ILLUSTRATIONS.

		PAGE
VIGNETTE—St. Michael's Mount	...*Title-page.*	
1. Querqueville Church		6
2. Plan of Querqueville Church		6
3. Château of Tourlaville		9
4. Castle of Bricquebec		13
5. Badge of the Sœurs de la Miséricorde		17
6. Coutances Cathedral		20
7. Pilaster and Cornice from Tomb of Bp. James in Cathedral of Dol		31
8. Front of the Tomb		32
9. Menhir, near Dol		35
10. Château of Combourg		37
11. Peasant Girl of Cancale		38
12. St. Malo and Chateaubriand's Tomb		40
13. Effigy of Jean de Beaumanoir		52
14. Château of La Bellière		54
15. Chimney, Château of La Bellière		56
16. Château of La Garaye		60
17. Section of Lanleff Church		69
18. Plan of Lanleff Church		70
19. Fountain of Duke Peter		73
20. Abbey of Beauport		77
21. Skull-box		91
22. The Creisker		107
23. Calvary, Guimiliau		116
24. The Fool's Well, Folgoët		124
25. Abbey of St. Mathieu		131
26. Peasant Girl of Ouëssant		133
27. Peasant Girl, Châteaulin		135
28. Begger, Quimper		141
29. Concarneau, with Sardine Boats		143
30. Dolmen, Trégunc		146
31. Rocking-Stone, Trégunc		148

		PAGE
32.	Château of Rustéphan	150
33.	Scala Sancta, Ste. Anne d'Auray	159
34.	Champ des Martyrs, Auray	169
35.	Sculptured Stone, Locmariaker	171
36.	Hatchet-shaped Sculpture, Locmariaker	173
37.	Entrance to Tumulus of Gavr' Inis	175
38, 39.	Sculptured Stones, Gavr' Inis	176
40.	Dolmen of Corcorro	182
41.	Castle of Elven	200
42.	Column of the Thirty	206
43.	Château of Josselin	212
44.	Salt-Pans, with Le Croisic in the distance	235
45.	Paludier of the Bourg de Batz in his working dress	237
46.	Paludier of the Bourg de Batz in his wedding dress	239
47.	La Roche Bernard	247
48.	Entrance to Le Palais, Belle Isle	253
49.	Device of Fouquet	257
50.	Peasant Girl, Pont l'Abbé	258
51.	Apse of the Church, Loctudy	260
52.	Torche of Penmarch	262
53.	Ship sculptured on the walls, Church of St. Guenolé, Penmarch	264
54.	Church of Guenolé, Penmarch	265
55.	Fleur-de-lisé Window, Church of St. Nonna, Penmarch	269
56.	Pointe du Raz	270
57.	Front of the Church at Pont Croix	277
58.	Wheel of Sacring Bells, Notre Dame-de-Comfort, near Douarnenez	279
59.	Costume of a Finistère Bride	281
60.	Well of Ste. Anne-la-Palue	284
61.	Cross Stones	286
62.	Rood-screen or Jubé, St. Fiacre	291
63.	Carved Stalls, St. Herbot	304
64.	Carved Stalls, St. Herbot	305

BRITTANY AND ITS BYWAYS.

A FAIR wind conveyed us in six hours from Poole to Cherbourg. It was dusk when we entered the harbour, and so we had no opportunity of seeing its beauty until the following morning, when we ascended a height behind the town, called the Mont du Roule. It is reached either on foot or by carriage, the Emperor having ordered a road to be made up to the fort which crowns the heights, on the occasion of the visit to Cherbourg, in 1858, of her Majesty Queen Victoria. Some 1500 men were immediately set to work, and, in a few days, an easy carriage-road was finished, up which the Emperor drove the Queen at his usual rapid pace. The view from the fort is lovely, commanding the whole line of the northern point of the Cotentin, from the low promontory of Cape de la Hogue to Barfleur. The water of the harbour, owing to its great depth, is of the most intense blue, which we quite agreed with the guardian of the fort in likening to that of the Bay of Naples. Across its entrance stretches, for two miles, the long line of the breakwater, and within were anchored the fleet of our yacht squadron, which the day before had run a race between Poole and Cherbourg. We took a boat to visit the breakwater. It is commanded at each end by a fort, with another in the centre, where the provisions are kept. In stormy weather the sea washes over the breakwater, and sometimes for days prevents all communication between the forts, and the supplies consequently are stopped. Boys offered us for sale the silvery shells of the Venus' ear, which inhabits the rocks of the breakwater. We afterwards saw them in the fish-market exposed for sale, and, on expressing some curiosity as to how they were eaten, the landlord had a dish prepared for us. These fish resemble the scallop in taste, but are very tough, and require a great deal of beating with a wooden mallet to make them tender enough to eat. They are called "ormer," or "gofish." The table d'hôte was very plentifully supplied with fish, and here, as throughout Normandy and Brittany, cider, the customary beverage of the country, was always placed upon the table. It varies very much in quality in different districts; that of Bayeux is most esteemed.

The next morning we set out for the dockyard. To obtain admission, it first requires a letter from the English Consul, who lives in a charming spot overlooking the sea, at the foot of the Montagne du Roule. Furnished with this, we repaired to the Préfet Maritime, who gave us an order to be presented at the dockyard gate, where it was countersigned, and a guide appointed to show us over the establishment. We made the tour round all the basins and workshops, and saw the canot impérial used by the Emperor on the visit of our Queen,— a most elegant boat, beautifully carved with marine subjects. The model of a Roman trireme, or galley, is in one of the basins, and in the little museum, or Salle des Modèles, are the two flagstones that covered the grave of Napoleon, and were deposited here by the Prince de Joinville, when he returned with the Emperor's remains from St. Helena. The dockyard partly stands on a spot called Chantereyne. The Empress Matilda, fleeing from Stephen, was overtaken by a tempest when making for Cherbourg, and vowed, if her life were spared, to build a church. The ship was in jeopardy, but the pilot cheered her spirits, and, when gaining the port, exclaimed, "Chantes Reine! we are safe in harbour." The place where she landed has always retained the name; and here the Empress, in fulfilment of her vow, founded an abbey, which was destroyed in the Revolution. The habitations of the nuns is the present provisional Hôpital de la Marine; a new one, containing above a thousand beds, being in course of construction, and a modern church, called Eglise du Vœu, has been erected in another part of the town in place of that of the Empress Matilda.

Henry II. held his court in the castle with his empress-mother in great splendour; it had formerly been tenanted by Duke William of Normandy before his invasion of England, and, within its enclosure, he built a church also, in consequence of a vow made during a serious illness. There are few objects of interest in the town of Cherbourg. The women all wear the large Normandy cap. In the Place d'Armes is a bronze equestrian statue of the Emperor Napoleon I., and on the pedestal is inscribed "J'avois résolu de renouveler à Cherbourg les merveilles de l'Egypte." In the Library is a curiously sculptured chimney-piece of the fifteenth century, coloured and gilt, removed from a room of the abbey. The principal church, La Trinité, is a strange jumble of architecture. There is some beautiful tracery in the windows, and a fine boss (clef pendante) in the south porch, now restored. On a board in the church is an inscription, setting forth it was built in consequence of a "vœu solennel des habitans de Cherbourg en 1450 de la délivrance de la domination étrangère"—that is, from the English, whose defeat the same year at Formigny, by the Constable de Richemont, expelled them for ever from Normandy.

There is much to see in the environs of Cherbourg, which makes it a good central point for excursions. We drove by the fort of Octeville, where a magnificent panoramic view is obtained, equalling in extent that from the Mont du Roule. A fisherman, who was standing by, told us the names of the numerous forts that bristle in every direction, and related to us the legend of the monk of Saire, who, having received the rent due to his father for some land, appropriated the money to his own use, and, on the tenant declaring he had paid the sum, adjured the evil one to carry him off, if he had ever received the money. The words were no sooner uttered than there came a flash of lightning, and the monk vanished: but he still appears in the roads of Cherbourg floating on the sea; when he sees a sailor, he cries "Save me, save me! I am about to sink!" but the hapless being who approaches to assist him is immediately dragged into the water, a peal of infernal laughter is heard, and the luckless mariner disappears for ever. We asked our guide if he believed in the phantom monk, but he was silent.

From Octeville we proceeded to Querqueville, where, in the same churchyard as the parochial church, stands a little church, named after St. Germain, the first apostle of the Cotentin, who, in the fifth century, landed from England on the coast of La Hogue, and preached Christianity in this district and the valley traversed by the river Saire, which falls into the sea near St. Vaast-la-Hogue. This tiny church, for it measures only 34 feet by 24, and is 11 feet high, is by some supposed to have been a

1. Querqueville Church.

temple of the Gauls converted into a Christian place of worship; the nave and tower having been added to the old temple, which consists of a triple apse forming

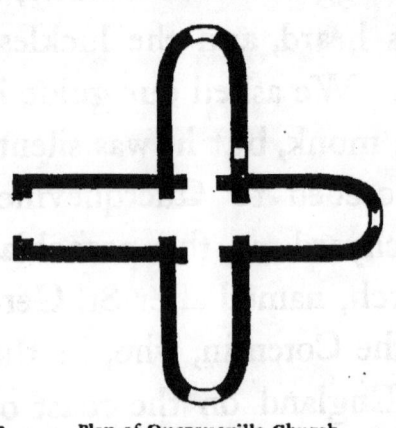

2. Plan of Querqueville Church.

a regular trefoil, each of which has a domed top. We drove on to Nacqueville, the château of Comte Hippolyte de Tocqueville. The park is prettily laid out, a stream of water runs in front of the house, and a row of blue hydrangeas blazed forth in great beauty, with the relief of a background of dark firs. Time prevented us from pursuing our excursion further west, to see the famed cliffs of Jobourg.

To the east of Cherbourg a high road leads to Barfleur and the lighthouse of Gatteville, between which and the Isle of Wight is the narrowest point of the English Channel, passing by Saint-Pierre-Eglise, near which is the château of the late Alexis de Tocqueville, author of 'Democracy in America;' but we did not get further on the road than Tourlaville, the ancient château of the Ravalet family, upon whom tradition has heaped every crime imaginable. One seigneur entered the church with his hounds and stabbed the priest at the altar, because he refused to administer to him the consecrated element; another hanged some of his vassals, because they did not grind their corn at the seignorial mill, for "haute or basse justice" was then among the nobles' rights. Marguerite, a daughter of this ancient house, expiated, with her brother, their offences upon the scaffold at Paris. Every effort was made to spare their lives; but the King, or rather Queen Margot, was inexorable. The château of Tourlaville is beautifully situated; it is in the style of the Renaissance, with an angular tower, which recals that of Heidelberg Castle. The ground-floor consists of two large unfurnished rooms, and a staircase, with iron railing, leads to the story above. In one room hangs the portrait of a lady châteleine, in the costume of the period of Louis XIII., with the château of Tourlaville in the distance. On her left are eight Cupids with bandages over their eyes, one in advance of the others is not blinded. From the lady's mouth is a label, with the inscription " Un (seul) me suffit." This is said to be the portrait of the Lady Marguerite, but the costume is of a later date. In one of the rooms is a chimney-piece covered with a variety of amatory devices and mottoes:—a Cupid blinded, holding a lighted torch, motto " Ce qui me donne la vie me cause la mort." Again, another Cupid with eyes bandaged, pouring water out of a vase to cool a flaming heart he holds in his hand, motto " Sa froideur me glace les veines et son ardeur brûle mon cœur." Six winged hearts flying at the approach of Cupid, but which are reached by his darts, " Même en fuyant l'on est pris." Further is a sentiment in verse :—

> " Plusieurs sont atteints de ce feu,
> Mais il ne s'en guérit que fort peu."

Again,—

> " Ces deux n'en font qu'un."

A river in the foreground, in the distance a setting sun, motto " Ainsi puissai-je mourir." This assemblage of devices and mottoes is not applicable to any particular individual, but may be supposed to be merely an expression of the taste of the time. They are of the seventeenth century, when the Ravalet had been succeeded by the Franquetot family, who have since taken the name of Coigny.

Château of Tourlaville.

Their arms, with several others, are in the little boudoir in one of the towers, called the Blue Chamber. Its walls are distempered blue, and the coverlet and hangings of the bed, with all the decorations of the room, are of the same colour. Having admired the lovely view from the "Tour des quatre vents," we descended to the kitchen of the farmer who rents the house, which now belongs to the Tocqueville family. His wife was busily employed in making "crêpes," a favourite kind of cake in Normandy and Brittany. It is made generally of the flour of the sarrasin or buckwheat, mixed with milk or water, and spread into a kind of pancake, which is fried on an iron pan, resembling the Scotch griddle-cakes. Another variety, called "galette," is made of the same ingredients, but differs from the crêpe in its being made three or four times the thickness, and is therefore not so light. Though generally made of buckwheat, wheat or oat-flour is sometimes used; and in the towns, sugar and cinnamon and vanilla are added, and the simple character of the crêpe entirely changed under the hands of the confectioner. The little village of Tourlaville was famous for its glassworks, until supplanted by those of Gobain.

On our return to Cherbourg we visited the lace school of the Sœurs de la Providence, where about two hundred girls are employed in making black lace like that of Bayeux, which has now completely superseded the Chantilly; the manner of making both laces is similar. The old Chantilly has completely died out, and the modern manufacture extends the whole length of Normandy from Cherbourg to Bayeux. How the children can keep the bobbins from entangling is a marvel; there were as many as five hundred on one pillow. The lace-makers were chiefly employed in flounces, shawls, and other large works. These are all made in separate pieces, and united by the stitch called fine joining or "raboutissage." A half-shawl or "pointe" was divided into thirty segments. We passed the evening at the Etablissement, and next morning left Cherbourg.

The railway traverses the picturesque and rocky valley of Quincampoix to Martinvast, whose little Romanesque church stands close to the station, and at a short distance is the château of Martinvast, where its late proprietor, M. du Moncel, established a model farm. A monument has been erected to his memory in the church by the commune of Martinvast.

At Sottevast we took the omnibus for Bricquebec, which lies nearly five miles from the station. Its ruined castle, dating from the end of the fourteenth century, with its lofty octagonal donjon, nearly a hundred feet high, standing on a high "motte" or artificial mound, has a most imposing appearance. Bricquebec, the most considerable demesne of the

4.   Castle of Bricquebec.

Cotentins, was taken by King Henry V. from the Sire d'Estouteville, who had so gallantly defended Mont St. Michel against him. Henry gave Bricquebec to William de la Pole, Earl of Suffolk, the ill-fated favourite of Queen Margaret of Anjou, and he, on being taken prisoner by the French, sold it, to raise the money for his ransom, to Sir Bertie Entwistle, who fought at Agincourt, and who held it till the battle of Formigny expelled the English from Normandy, and Sir Bertie fell at St. Albans in the Lancastrian cause. The inn, "Hôtel du Vieux Château," is within the enclosure of the ruins—a most dilapidated old place; our dirty ill-furnished room next to a hayloft, the horses passing through the house to the stable, and every kind of litter and rubbish accumulated under the windows. Yet in the room we occupied had once slept our gracious Sovereign Queen Victoria. On a placard is inscribed, "Chambre de la famille royale d'Angleterre, 18 Août 1857;" and below stairs is another, setting forth, "S. M. la Reine d'Angleterre, le Prince Albert, les Princesses Royale et Alice, le Prince Alfred, sont descendus à l'hôtel du Vieux Château le 10 Août 1857." About a mile from Bricquebec is a Trappist convent; but we were not allowed admission beyond the parlour, where is sold a quantity of cutlery, not made—as we were given to understand when offered for sale—by the monks.

Regaining the railroad, we went on to Valognes, which has been styled the St. Germain of Normandy; a dull town, with worn-out houses, occupied by worn-out aristocratic families. The grass grows in the streets.

Here we left the rail and proceeded to Saint

Sauveur-le-Vicomte. On entering the town, the castle is on the right of the road, the Abbey church on the left. The large demesne of Saint Sauveur-le-Vicomte passed by marriage into the Harcourt family, and belonged, in the time of Edward III., to Geoffrey d'Harcourt, whose fortress was one of the most formidable in Normandy. Banished from France, he went over to England and persuaded Edward III. to make a descent upon Normandy instead of Gascony, assuring him he would find rich towns and fair castles without any means of defence, and that his people would gain wealth enough to suffice them for twenty years to come. The King landed at La Hogue, or Saint Vaast-la-Hogue, as it is now called, where he knighted the Prince of Wales and made Warwick and Harcourt marshals of his army. They advanced in three divisions—the King and the Prince in the centre, the two marshals on the right and left—ravaging all before them, and not stopping in their victorious course till the great victory at Crecy. Harcourt subsequently met a traitor's fate. A force was sent against him, his army was routed, and, preferring death to being taken, he fought most valiantly until he was struck to the ground by French lances, when some men-at-arms dispatched him with their swords. He had sold the reversion of his castle to King Edward III., to whom it was confirmed by the treaty of Bretigny. Edward bestowed the barony upon that pride of English chivalry, Sir John Chandos, in recompense for his great services in the wars. The square donjon and inner gate were built by Chandos. The castle is well preserved, and is now used as a hospice for orphans and aged women. The rooms are kept beautifully clean, and on a tablet in one of the corridors is written up " Dortoirs restaurés par la munificence de M. le Comte Georges d'Harcourt en mémoire de ses illustres ayeux, anciens Seigneurs de ce château, en 1838."

The Benedictine convent also belonged to the Harcourts until the revolt of Geoffrey. It is now the property of the Sœurs de la Miséricorde, who have rebuilt the fine Abbey church according to its former model. Originally built in the eleventh century, it was partly burnt in the fourteenth, and reconstructed in the fifteenth. The columns and arches of the nave are of the first period; the form of the church is a Latin cross, having an apse ornamented with a double row of lancet windows, richly sculptured. The sculptures are all executed by an untaught workman of the place, who died before he had completed the pulpit. To collect the funds necessary for the undertaking, the foundress travelled throughout Europe. Her tomb is in the church. "Julie Françoise Catherine Postel, née à Barfleur, 1756. Sœur Marie Madelaine, Fondatrice et première Supérieure Générale de l'Institut des Ecoles Chrétiennes de la Miséricorde, morte en odeur de Sainteté 16 Juillet 1846, à l'Abbaye de St. Sauveur-le-Vicomte." The badge of the sisterhood is a cross inscribed with their motto " L'obéissance jusqu'à la mort." Some of the party made an attempt at fishing in the little river Douve, but without success, though rewarded for their walk by a pretty view of the apse of the Abbey church, with its delicately-sculptured lancet windows, from the opposite side of the river.

5.

We hired a private carriage (*voiture à volonté*) to Périers. After passing over a hilly road we crossed a marsh which extends from Carentan to the sea, and reached a town called La Haye-du-Puits—a singular name derived from the custom in the middle ages of surrounding the " motte " or enclosure upon which the donjon was built, with a wooden palisade, or sometimes with a thick hedge formed of thorns and branches of trees interlaced: hence La Haye-du-Puits, La Haye-Pesnel, and others. Here is a Norman church restored: all the capitals of the columns are of the same pattern.

The Abbey church at Lessay, where next we

stopped, is of the twelfth century, and considered, with Coutances and Périers, to be the finest examples of Romanesque in the Cotentin. The arches are round, and all the architecture of the church, which has been restored, is of the same period. The Abbey of Lessay had transmarine jurisdiction and the right of presentation to the Priory of Boxgrove and other endowments in the diocese of Chichester. The Abbey house, now inhabited, is a fine modernised habitation. At Lessay we saw the manner of washing linen practised in many places throughout Normandy and Brittany. Being first roughly washed in the river, the clothes are placed in layers in a large cask, with a bunghole at the bottom, alternately with wood-ashes, and on the top is laid a piece of coarse sacking. Boiling water is poured over the top, which, as it passes through the linen, absorbs the soda of the ashes, escaping at the bottom and carrying away with it all impurities. This process is repeated several times till the clothes are perfectly white.

Throughout this part of the country the mistletoe hangs as the sign of a cabaret; and if cider is sold, some apples are fastened to the bush. On the road to Périers we crossed a "lande" or common, where we met numerous carts carrying sea sand, here used to mix with the heavy soil as manure.

At Périers we slept at the little inn "La Croix

Blanche," kept by Madame Casimir, the widow of a Polish officer, well known for her eccentricity and good cuisine. The entrance to the apartments in the inns is generally through the kitchen; in many the box bedstead (*lit clos*) stands in the corner near the fire, Breton fashion. On a barber's shop we saw painted up "Içi l'on rajeunit." The church has a tall spire, and is one of the finest religious edifices in this part of Normandy—painted windows, the capitals of the columns of varied foliage, and fine groined clustered arches.

We had a most perilous drive to Coutances, the coachman, "en ribote," drove us at a fearful pace, and we were thankful when we arrived in safety. The Norman cathedral is beautiful—so simple, so pure, and elegant; its tall towers terminating in spires; and the chapels being separated by open mullioned arches, great lightness is given to the interior. The Bishop of Coutances was officiating at the consecration of some stones for a new pavement; each flag was rubbed over and anointed with oil.

The church of St. Pierre has a handsome square tower, pierced gallery, and apse with a double row of columns. In the church of St. Nicholas we particularly noticed the fine bosses of the groined arches in the chancel. The fonts hereabouts have the serpent with the apple, and the cross carved upon the cover. The church was filled with pots of flowers they were employed in removing, for the day before

6. Coutances Cathedral.

had been the Fête of St. Fiacre, the patron of gardeners. St. Fiacre, or Fiaker, was an Irish monk of the seventh century, who, according to tradition, obtained from the Bishop of Meaux a grant of as much ground out of the forest as he could dig a trench round in one day's labour, for the purpose of making a garden and cultivating vegetables for travellers. Long time after, the peasants would show the ditch ten times longer than was expected, and relate how, when the Irishman took his stick to trace a line upon the soil, the earth dug itself under the point of the stick, while the forest trees fell right and left to save him the trouble of cutting them down. Outside the town are the remains of an aqueduct, with ivy-covered arches, said to be the work of the middle ages. It is a good point of view for sketching the cathedral, and the public gardens also command a fine prospect.

The approach to Granville is by a sharp descent. The town is built at the foot of a rocky promontory, the streets rising in terraces cut in the rock, on the top of which are the citadel and the church on the culminating point. It has been styled a Gibraltar in miniature. A fort was built here by Lord Scales, who commanded the English forces in the Cotentin in the time of Henry VI., and it was taken by surprise by Estouteville, the hero of Saint Michel. The church is cruciform in plan, the arms of the cross being equal. The axis of the nave is inclined to the left, as we afterwards observed that of the Creisker at St. Pol de Léon. It has been lately restored, and the painted windows are offerings of the different families of the town. The view from the top of the "Roc" is very extensive, including the Chausey islands and Jersey. A steamer runs twice a week to St. Helier. A deep cutting in the rocks opens on the beach, where the bathing-machines are stationed—curious little canvas huts carried upon poles, like sedan chairs. The tide here rises 45 feet. It was to Granville the Vendean army, commanded by La Rochejacquelin, appointed generalissimo at twenty-two, marched after their fatal step of crossing the Loire, expecting to make a junction with the English; but Granville was vigorously defended, contrary winds retarded the arrival of the English fleet, and the retreat from the coast, where it might have been supported by the English, was the ruin of the Royalist army. Of the 80,000 who crossed the Loire sixty days before, only 8000 remained to make their last heroic resistance at Savenay, which ended the great Vendean war. A few months after, the hero of this noble army, the chivalrous Henri de la Rochejacquelin, fell from the bullet of a soldier whose life he had spared[1]:—

> "Lorsqu'en des jours trop malheureux
> Pâlissait l'astre de la France ;
> Quand les cœurs les plus valeureux
> Semblaient perdre toute espérance,

[1] "Si je recule, tuez-moi; si j'avance, suivez-moi; si je meurs, vengez-moi," was his celebrated address to the peasant army.

L'antique honneur, la sainte foi,
Brillèrent dans cette contrée ;
Mourir pour son Dieu, pour son roi,
Fut le serment de la Vendée."

The costume of the Granville women is singular. They wear long black cloaks or mantles, edged with a frill of the same material, and on their heads a kind of bandeau or under-cap, turned up at the ears, surmounted by a white handkerchief, folded square and placed horizontally upon the head, like the plinth of a Grecian capital.

We drove to St. Pair, a small watering-place about two miles from Granville, nicely situated in a little sandy bay. In the middle of the church is the monumental tomb of St. Pair and another saint (St. Gault); their effigies, with mitre and crozier, side by side.

Next day we had a beautiful drive to Avranches. A winding road leads up to the town, which is situated on an elevated plateau, commanding a view of Brittany on one side and of Normandy on the other—a broad expanse of land and sea, the former extending over the valley of the Sée, with its network of small streams interlacing each other; Mont St. Michel appears in the distance. The finest view is from the Botanic gardens. The cathedral of Avranches fell at the end of the last century, but a model of it is preserved in the museum. One stone remains, carefully surrounded by massive chains, with an inscription recording that it was the spot where Henry II. received absolution for the murder of Thomas à Becket:—"Sur cette pierre, içi à la porte de la cathédrale d'Avranches, après le meurtre de Thomas Becket, Archévêque de Cantorbéry, Henri II., roi d'Angleterre, duc de Normandie, reçut à genoux, des légats du pape, l'absolution apostolique, le dimanche xxii Mai, 1172." The cemetery is at the foot of the hill; the tombs are of granite, with the letters in relief: among them we read many well-known English names.

At Pontorson we could find no remains of the castle of Du Guesclin, which was nearly surprised by the English under a captain named Felton, during the absence of Du Guesclin, with the connivance of the "chambrières" of the Lady Typhaine, his wife. Already their scaling-ladders were against the wall, when Juliana, Du Guesclin's sister, agitated by a troublous dream, awoke suddenly, seized a sword, rushed to the window, and upset three English who were coming up the ladder, and they were killed by the fall. The enemy retired. Next morning Du Guesclin, on his return to Pontorson, met Felton and his party, attacked them, and took them prisoners. When Typhaine saw Felton, she tauntingly exclaimed, "Comment, brave Felton, vous voilà encore! C'est trop pour un homme de cœur comme vous d'être battu, dans une intervalle de douze heures, une fois par la sœur, une autre par le frère." Du Guesclin caused the faithless " chambrières" to be sewed up in sacks and flung into the river.

John IV. Duke of Britanny conferred upon Du Guesclin the government of Pontorson, of which territory he was personally lord, by right of his mother. It was here he often resided, and here he celebrated being made Constable of France by King Charles V., and fraternised with Olivier de Clisson, agreeing to afford each other mutual help—" contre tous ceux qui peuvent vivre et mourir." The granite church was founded by Duke Robert, father of the Conqueror.

Pontorson is the most convenient place for visiting Mont St. Michel. Our drive thither was by the banks of the river Couësnon, along a sandy road, bordered on each side by hedges of tamarisks, which leads to the "Grève," or sands, which have to be crossed to reach the Mount, a distance of rather more than a mile. We met numbers of bare-legged half-clad women and children, bringing in the produce of their fishing, shrimps and cockles tied up in nets, and peasants with carts carrying in sea sand for dressing the land. The appearance of Mont St. Michel is very imposing, a cone of granite encircled by the sea. Above rises the fortress, surmounted by the church, a height of 400 feet from the top to the water. Below, at the foot of the Mount, picturesquely situated on an insulated rock, is the little chapel of St. Aubert, Bishop of Avranches, the founder of St. Michel. The Mount has been the residence of many of our English princes. Matilda, queen of the Conqueror, visited St. Michel. It was here her son Henry I., then only Count of the Cotentin, was blockaded by his brothers William and Robert, and obliged to surrender. Here Henry II. held his court, and, when Henry V. overran Normandy, St. Michel was the only fortress that held out against him, under its gallant defender Louis d'Estouteville of Bricquebec. Two cannons, now at the entrance of the castle, are said to have been taken from the English at the siege. Normandy was always the scene of the quarrels between the English Norman princes, of the disputes between the sons of the Conqueror, between Stephen of Blois and Henry of Anjou, and again of those between Henry II. and his sons, and of Richard and his brother John, to the latter of whom the Normans were attached.

Seven French kings have made pilgrimages to St. Michel; and here Louis XI. instituted the order of knighthood, called in honour of the archangel St. Michael, but afterwards styled the order of the Coquille, from the cockleshells that formed the collar of the knights, and the golden cockle-shells that bordered their mantles. The motto of the order was the old motto of the Mount, "Immensi tremor Oceani" (the trembling of the immeasurable ocean), being an allusion to the popular belief that when the English approached St. Michel, the guardian archangel of the Mount raised a tempest to drive the enemy's vessels upon the rocks. This belief may be traced back to the time when the island was occupied by the Druid priestesses, who were supposed to have the power of raising storms and stilling them by their magic arrows of gold.

We ascended by the flight of steps to the "Merveille," as the convent building is called, and well it deserves its name, from its elegance, its boldness, and its position, with a wall of above one hundred feet high, and of immense length, rising from the rock and supported by fifteen buttresses, and divided into three stories. In every point of view it is one of the most remarkable edifices of the thirteenth century. The salle des chevaliers, where the chapters of the knights were held, is a fine hall, with three rows of columns, and above it are the beautiful Gothic cloisters. The "préau" or court is surrounded by a double row of pointed arches, interlacing each other, and filled in with flowered spandrils and cornices, carved with the greatest delicacy and endless variety. The church which crowns the building is supported by a circle of enormous columns in the crypt beneath, called the Souterrain des Gros Piliers: it has been entirely restored, and the carvings are the work of the prisoners who were confined here. From one of the doors we went out to the platform or terrace called Beauregard, from the beauty of its prospect, or sometimes Sault Gautier, from a prisoner of that name, who three times threw himself off the platform to commit suicide. The view from hence is most extensive, the whole circuit of the bay extending to the west as far as Cancale. In 1203 St. Michel became a royal demesne, and the buildings were entirely reconstructed by the Abbot Jourdan, assisted by Philip Augustus; and the works were continued by his successors to 1260.

Beneath and adjacent to the Mount, is the little island of La Tombeleine or tombeau d'-Hélène, so called from a young lady of that name, who unable to accompany her lover knight when he left for England with the Conqueror, as soon as the vessel which carried him away disappeared from her sight, laid down on the shore and died. Every year, on the anniversary of her death, the fishermen will tell you they see a dove seated upon the Tombeleine rock, and remain there till morning's dawn.

The guide pointed out to us the window of St. Michel, from which Barbès tried to escape by means of a cord made of his sheets cut into strips and tied together; but the line was too short, and he fell upon the rock and was taken up much hurt. The provisions for the fortress are brought in up an inclined plane, and raised by means of a tread-wheel, formerly worked by the prisoners. We were conducted to the spot where stood, with bars only three inches apart, the iron cage in which so many celebrities were immured. Dubourg, the Dutch journalist, who wrote against Louis XIV., died within its bars, devoured, it is said, by the rats. In 1777, the Comte d'Artois (afterwards Charles X.) desired it should be destroyed, but his wishes were disregarded. His cousin, the Duc de Chartres (afterwards Louis Philippe), with his brother and sister, and Madame de Genlis, subsequently visited the Mount. All exclaimed against the iron cage, and when they heard that the Comte d'Artois had ordered its destruction, they sent for hatchets, and the Duc de Chartres gave the first blow towards its demolition; but the fine old fortress is no longer desecrated as a prison. The Emperor has restored it to its original position, and it is now placed under the control of the Bishop of Coutances, and is used as an asylum for orphans under the care of a few Sisters.

Next morning we crossed the boundary between Normandy and Brittany, the river Couësnon, which has often changed its course, once, it is said, running beyond St. Michel—hence the popular saying—

" Le Couësnon par sa folie
A mis le Mont en Normandie."

We had a beautiful drive to Dol or Dol-de-Bretagne, as it is styled, to distinguish it from the fortress of the same name in the Jura, upon the taking of which Madame de Sevigné writes in her letters with so much enthusiasm. We were now fairly in Brittany, which though geographically part of France still remains very distinct, owing to the Celtic origin of its inhabitants. Brittany consists of five departments; but it is in Lower Brittany alone, comprised in the departments of Finistère, Morbihan, and the Côtes-du-Nord, that the true Celtic race, its language, names, features, costumes, and superstitions are to be found.

This is the true Brittany, the Bretagne Bretonnante of Froissart, who calls the eastern part of the province, La Bretagne Douce, because the French language is spoken there. Dol was the great bulwark of Brittany against Normandy; the wall and moat surrounding the town, with some of the towers, still remain. Many of the houses are built, as the French term it, "en colombage" that is, with the upper story projecting some fifteen feet over the ground-floor, forming a gallery or porch supported by oak posts or columns with sculptured capitals of the thirteenth century. The inn we occupied had one of these porches: Madame Barbot, our landlady, and her maid, were both dressed in Breton costume, with lace-trimmed embroidered caps and aprons of fine muslin, clear-starched and ironed with a perfection which the most accomplished "blanchisseuse du fin" of Paris would find it difficult to surpass. The people here have the Breton physiognomy, sharp black eyes, short round faces and brown freckled complexions, a contrast to the blue eyes, long oval faces, and bright tints of their Norman neighbours.

The principal building at Dol is the Cathedral, built of grey granite, in the style of many of our English churches. On the south is the "porte episcopale," a large projecting porch with mullioned sides, and, near it, a smaller porch with a central column semée of hearts, the "armes parlantes" of Bishop Cœuret who built it. The clustered columns of the nave, consist of a central pillar surrounded by four others running up to the roof, so slender and delicate that they are united to the centre by small bars of iron. Over the high altar is an enormous wooden crozier, carved and gilt, from which the Host is suspended.

7. Pilaster and Cornice from the Tomb of Bishop James, Cathedral, Dol.

A beautiful Renaissance tomb on the north side of the cathedral was raised in 1507 to the memory of Bishop James, who died three years before. The sculpture is much mutilated, but the arabesques are most delicately and elegantly chiselled. It is supposed to be the work of Jean Just of Tours, sculptor of the magnificent tomb of Louis XII. and Anne of Brittany, erected at St. Denis by order of Francis I.

8.   Front of the Tomb of Bishop James, Cathedral, Dol.

The chapel of St. Samson, patron saint of the cathedral, has been restored. Mad people were brought here for cure, and placed in a recess which still remains; the opening was covered over by an iron grating. Dol was formerly the ecclesiastical metropolis of Brittany; the see was founded by Samson, one of those British monks, who, with a whole population of men and women, emigrated from England to escape the Saxon slavery. They crossed the Channel in barks made of skins sewn together, singing, as they went, the Lamentations of the Psalmist. This emigration lasted more than a century (from 450 to 550), and poured a Christian population into a Celtic country where paganism was longest preserved. St. Samson and his six suffragans—all monks, missionaries, and bishops, like himself—were called the " Seven Saints of Brittany ; " St. Samson was what was termed an "evêque portatif," meaning a bishop without a diocese, until he founded that of Dol. Telio, also a British monk, with the assistance of St. Samson, planted near Dol an orchard three miles in length, and to him is attributed the first introduction of the apple-tree into Brittany. Wherever the monks went, they cultivated the soil; all had in their mouths the words of the Apostle, "If any would not work, neither should he eat." The people admired the industry of the new comers, and, from admiration they passed to imitation; the peasants joined the monks in tilling the ground, and even the brigands became agriculturists. "The Cross and the plough, labour and prayer," was the motto of these early missionaries.

> "Sûr que le Ciel maudit l'arbre stérile,
> Le sage passe en opérant le bien :
> Vivre et mourir à l'univers utile,
> C'est la devise et l'esprit du chrétien."
> *Chants de Piété*, MALO DE GARABY.

The monks of Dol were great bee-farmers, as we learn from an anecdote told by Count Montalembert in his 'Moines de l'Occident.' One day when St Samson of Dol and St. Germain, Bishop of Paris, were conversing on the respective merits of their monasteries, St. Samson said that his monks were such good and careful preservers of their bees that, besides the honey which they yielded in abundance, they furnished more wax than was used in the churches during the year, but that, their climate not being fit for the growth of vines, they had great scarcity of wine. Upon hearing this, St. Germain replied, "We, on the contrary, produce more wine than we can consume, but we have to buy wax; so, if you will furnish us with wax, we will give you a tenth of our wine." Samson accepted the offer, and the mutual arrangement was continued during the lives of the two saints.

The marshy country round Dol has been formerly inundated by the sea; it is now reclaimed and protected by a dyke twenty-two miles long, extending from Pontorson to Chateauneuf. The whole tract is full of buried wood, a submerged forest, which the people dig up, and use for furniture. It is black, like the Irish bog-oak. They call it "couëron." In the midst of this plain rises a mamelon or insulated granite rock, resembling in form Mont St. Michel, called the Mont Dol. On the top is the little chapel of Notre Dame de l'Espérance, upon which was formerly a telegraph, and near it is a column surmounted by a colossal statue of Our Lady. Mont Dol was a consecrated place of the Druids. The guides showed us a spring which

9. Menhir, near Dol.

never dries, and also a rock upon which they point out the print of the foot of the demon, left by him when wrestling with St. Michael. We met the curé, who gave us a medal of the church, and told us the principal points in the view before us, extending over the whole Bay of Cancale.

On our way back to Dol, we walked to a cornfield, in the midst of it stands a menhir[1] (they are so termed from the Breton *mœn*, stone, and *hir*, long), called the "Pierre du champ dolant," a shaft of gray granite, about thirty feet high, and said to measure fifteen more underground. On the top is a cross. The first preachers of Christianity, unable to uproot the veneration for the menhirs, surmounted them with the cross, preserving the worship but changing the symbol. In the same manner, they did not attempt to destroy the veneration for sacred groves and fountains, but transferred to new saints the miracles of times past.

We drove through a pretty country to see the Château of Combourg, where Chateaubriand passed his early days. It is a fine square castle of the fifteenth century, with massive towers at each corner, surrounded by trees, and standing proudly over the village below. The drawbridge has been replaced by a modern "perron" or flight of stone steps, which leads to the entrance hall. The salle d'honneur looks over a lake. We were taken into his little melancholy room which Chateaubriand so well describes.

---

[1] The largest menhir in Finistère is on a lande near the farm of Kergloas, or "the plain of mourning;" this, with the menhir of Dol, have probably been erected as funeral monuments, or point out the scene of some battle slaughter.

Dol — Cancale.

"La fenêtre de mon donjon s'ouvrait sur le cour intérieure; le jour, j'avais en perspective les créneaux de la courtine opposeé, où végétaient des scolopendres et croissait un prunier sauvage. Quelques martinets, qui, durant l'été, s'enfonçaient en criant dans les trous des murs, étaient mes seuls compagnons. La nuit je n'apercevais qu'un petit morceau du ciel et quelques étoiles. Lorsque la lune brillait et qu'elle s'abaissait à l'occident, j'en étais averti par ses rayons, qui venaient à mon lit au travers des carreaux losangés de la fenêtre. Des chouettes voletant d'un tour à l'autre, passant et repassant entre la lune et moi, dessinaient sur mes rideaux l'ombre mobile de leurs ailes."

10.   Château of Combourg.

The bed on which Chateaubriand died has been brought from Paris and placed in the room.

The next morning we left Dol for Cancale, of such world-wide celebrity for its oysters. We left the railway at La Gouesnière, five miles and a half from Cancale, to which we proceeded by the mail cart. It requires to travel in Brittany to form any notion of the detestable vehicles, whether public or "voitures à volonté," in which travellers in this country are condemned to ride. Uncleaned, unpainted, creaking, jolting machines—as fully tenanted with

Peasant Girl of Cancale.

every kind of insect annoyance, as if one were travelling in a hen-house. The horses are good, hardy, enduring little animals, which go their thirty to fifty miles a day without any distress either to themselves or the traveller. The Breton drivers are gentle and kind, making more use of their voices than of their whips in urging on their horses. The town of Cancale is situated on the heights, a precipitous descent leading to the village below, called La Houle, which lines the edge of the shore, and is occupied mostly by fishermen. This is the port, and here are the pier and the lighthouse, and also a comfortable inn to which the people of St. Malo resort in large parties, an omnibus running thence daily. The panoramic view of the bay of Cancale is beautiful and most extensive, one vast crescent of sand some ten square leagues in extent, stretching from the picturesque rocks of Cancale to Granville, its most northern point, and including Mont Dol, Mont St. Michel, and Avranches. The western side is lined with huts and windmills, but the water is so shallow that no boat can land. Having walked round the little hurdled-in oyster parks, numbering, we were told, about 600, and made ourselves very wet and dirty, though we borrowed sabots to enable us to wade through the mud, we returned to the inn, and next day reached St. Malo.

St. Malo stands on a small granite island at the mouth of the Rance, connected, by a causeway called " Le Sillon," with the mainland. The space it occupies is so small, that castle, churches, streets, and towers are all crowded together, and the whole is nearly surrounded by a sea wall, which makes the town appear as if rising straight out of the ocean. Towards the sea, the bay is encircled with groups of

12.   Tomb of Chateaubriand, and View of St. Malo.

craggy islets, many surmounted by forts, bristling up as the tide recedes, in every direction. Conspicuous among these island rocks is that called the

Grand Bé, chosen by Chateaubriand for his last resting-place, as he wished to be buried near the place of his birth. Singularly enough the name of the island "Bé" signifies a tomb. On his request being granted, Chateaubriand wrote to the Mayor of St. Malo.

"Enfin, Monsieur, j'aurai un tombeau, et je vous le devrai, ainsi qu'à mes bienveillants compatriotes. Vous savez, Monsieur, que je ne veux que quelques pieds de sable, une pierre de rivage sans ornement et sans inscription, une simple croix de fer, et une petite grille pour empêcher les animaux de me deterrer. La croix dira que l'homme réposant à ses pieds était un Chrétien; cela suffit à ma mémoire."

At low water, the island is accessible on foot. The tomb consists of a plain stone without inscription, surmounted by a granite cross, and is surrounded by an iron railing. It is placed on the edge of a rock, and is the resort of crowds of pilgrims.

"La vaste mer murmure autour de son cercueil."

The Hôtel de France is the house where Chateaubriand's family lived, and the room he occupied is filled with various memorials of him. The Chateaubriand arms hang upon the wall. They were given by St. Louis to an ancestor who was wounded and taken prisoner at the battle of Massoura. The King changed the peacock's plumes, previously borne by the family, to fleurs de lys on a field gules, with the proud motto "Mon sang teint les bannières de France." The tides here rise to between forty and fifty feet above low-water mark, so that the harbour is dry at low water, and is crossed on foot to go to St. Servan, the suburb on the opposite side.

We walked round the ramparts and were shown the little gate down which were sent every night the watch dogs of St. Malo, "chiens Anglais qui s'appelent dogues." Shut up during the day, they were let out at ten at night, and recalled in the morning to the sound of a copper trumpet, by their keeper, styled the "chiennetier." Enactments were made for their maintenance, called the "droit de chiennage." When let loose at night, a warning bell was rung to apprise the inhabitants, as they tore the legs of every one they met. Hence it used to be said "Il a été à St. Malo, les chiens lui ont rongé les mollets." In 1770, a naval officer trying to force a passage was attacked by a troop of these dogs prowling between St. Malo and St. Servan; his sword was useless as defence, and, exhausted, in despair he threw himself into the sea, but here he was followed by the dogs and torn to pieces. A few days after they were all destroyed by the municipality, and the custom of keeping them has been since discontinued. In an old map of St. Malo, or "Saint Malo de l'isle," as it was then styled, preserved in the Imperial Library at Paris, is laid down, near the "Sillon" a little sentry-box marked, "Corps-de-garde de nuit pour les chiens," and again, near the "Tour de la grande Porte," is the "Pont aux chiens." The date of the map is 1662. The arms of St. Malo till the seventeenth century were, on a field argent, a mastiff gules.

The castle dates principally from the Queen-Duchess Anne, and one of its massive towers, the "Qui qu'en grogne" is a memorial of her dauntless spirit. Twice crowned Queen of France, she was the only one of her line worthy of the ducal crown. The Bishop of St. Malo was temporal lord of the town, and maintained he held it direct from the Pope, as a fief of the Church, because it was built upon land where a convent formerly stood; and consequently the Duke of Brittany had no authority over it, either spiritual or temporal. Duke John V. began to build a castle, but the Bishop opposed himself to its construction, and the contest lasted on until the time of the Queen-Duchess Anne, who, in defiance of the Bishop, and to shew that she was and always would be sovereign of St. Malo, finished the fortress and caused the lofty inscription to be placed in raised letters upon the great tower: "Qui qu'en grogne, ainsi sera, c'est mon plaisir;"—so runs the legend, but unfortunately a similar story is told of Louis II., Duke of Bourbon.

On the opposite side of the mouth of the Rance

is Dinard, lately become a favourite watering-place; it has good sands, and houses and villas are rapidly rising up in every direction, and covering its granite hills.

The prettiest route to Dinan is by the little steamer which ascends the Rance, a lovely voyage, occupying about two hours. The banks one mixture of rocks, valleys, and verdure; the river now expanding into the width of a lake, now narrowing between its forest-clothed sides. After passing through a lock, and, winding our way through a narrow pass of rocky crags, we reached the bridge of Dinan; above us, the gigantic granite viaduct stretched across the valley, the town, with its feudal walls and castle, perched on its rocky heights over the river.

In the Grande Place is a miserable statue of Du Guesclin, who looks more like a wandering minstrel than the hero of Brittany and Constable of France. His life forms quite an historic romance. His future greatness was foretold by a prophetess; his wife, the Lady Tiphaine, was herself a fairy; his battles resemble those of the giants of old. Du Guesclin was born at Broons, and was the eldest of ten children and of great trouble to his parents. One day his mother dreamt she was in possession of a casket, containing portraits of herself and her lord, and on one side were set nine precious stones of lustrous beauty encircling one rough unpolished pebble. In her dream she carried the casket to a lapidary, and asked him to take out the rough stone as unworthy of such goodly company; but he advised her to allow it to remain, and subsequently it shone forth more brilliantly than the precious gems with which it was surrounded. The after superiority of Bertrand over the other nine children explained the dream.

It was in this "Place," where his statue now stands, the celebrated duel took place between Du Guesclin and an English knight, called by the Breton chroniclers Thomas of Cantorbéry. Dinan was at that time closely besieged by the Duke of Lancaster (1359), with the young Count de Montfort, and defended by Du Guesclin. A truce of forty days had been agreed upon, before the expiration of which Oliver, brother of Du Guesclin, rode out unarmed beyond the city walls, and was made prisoner by Thomas of Cantorbéry, who demanded a ransom of 1000 florins. On this news reaching Du Guesclin, he immediately repaired to the English camp, where he found the Duke of Lancaster playing chess with Sir John Chandos. They received him most cordially, and agreed that the dispute should be settled by a combat within the walls, the Duke of Lancaster consenting to preside. Victory declared in favour of Du Guesclin, who would have cut off the head of his adversary, had not the Duke of Lancaster interceded for his life. Cantorbéry was dragged upon a hurdle out of the lists, and condemned to pay 1000 florins to Oliver; his horse and armour were given to Bertrand, and the felon knight expelled the English army.

We drove to see the Castle of Montafilant, one of the apanages of the Rohan family, which passed with many others to the unfortunate Gilles de Bretagne, by his marriage with the heiress Françoise de Dinan. The castle is approached by a steep winding path, leading to the plateau upon which it stands. Before the use of firearms, its position rendered it impregnable. Of its seven towers, two only remain.

The story of Gilles de Bretagne forms the subject of a romance by the Vicomte Walsh. Though his conduct was not free from blame, his long captivity and tragic end have rendered this unfortunate prince an object of pity to posterity. Third son of Duke John V., he was reared with Henry VI. of England, and personally attached to the English; but he never was in league with England against his own country, and his uncle the Constable Richemont regarded him as the honour and hope of his house. His wife Françoise was the most beautiful and accomplished woman of her time, the " perle de noblesse, de gentilesse, et de savoir;" and moreover possessed of the rich inheritance of her uncle Bertrand de Dinan, of the Montafilant branch. She had been betrothed from her infancy to the Sire de Gavre, son of Guy, Comte de Laval; but her father died when she was only eight years old, and Gilles de Bretagne carried her off by force. Dissatisfied with his paternal inheritance, the lordship of Champtocé, he retired to Guildo, one of the châteaux of Françoise's dower, where he passed his time in company with his English archers. His withdrawal from court was represented to Duke Francis as the beginning of a revolt, by Arthur de Montauban, his bitterest enemy and a great favourite of the Duke. Gilles neglected his young wife, and she is reported, in an unguarded moment, to have said to Montauban, she would marry him "if her husband were to die." Duke Francis was determined to get rid of his brother, and Charles VII. was persuaded to assist him in his vile design. The King arrested Gilles on the charge of high treason, as being in correspondence with the English; and, in proof of the charge, his enemies produced forged letters from the King of England compromising the loyalty of Gilles. Charles gave him over to his brother for punishment. In vain were Gilles's supplications to the Duke, or the entreaties of the Constable, who went to Dinan and knelt to Francis to beg for the pardon of his brother. Equally fruitless his being acquitted at Rédon, from there being no proof of his guilt. The unfortunate Gilles was dragged from prison to prison, and consigned to keepers destitute of every feeling of humanity. Montauban, an Italian by descent (his mother was a Visconti), sent for poison from Lombardy, and administered in his soup a strong dose, which the good constitution of Gilles enabled him to resist. Starvation was then tried, and the wretched Gilles would stand at his prison window, calling on the passers by to give him bread: "Du pain, du pain pour l'amour de Dieu," but no one ventured to relieve him. At last, a poor woman dared to give him food, and placed a loaf on the edge of his grated window, continuing for six months to share with him in secret her scanty meal of black bread. Seeing that he could hold out no longer and that his death was determined upon, Gilles begged the woman would fetch him a minister of religion, that he might confess before he died. By stealth she brought him a Cordelier monk, who confessed him across the bars of his prison, and Gilles adjured him to seek his brother and acquaint him with his pitiable condition. The monk started on his errand, but in the mean time the gaolers of Gilles determined on putting an end to his life. They twisted a cloth round his neck, and smothered him between two mattresses while he slept. The monks of Bosquen carried his body to their abbey for interment, and the wooden effigy that was placed over his grave is still preserved in the Museum at St. Brieuc. The monk who had received Gilles's confession went in quest of Duke Francis, who, on hearing of his brother's death when at Avranches, had left for Saint Michel. The monk met him on the Grève, and cited him in the name of his brother "de la part du Messire Gilles" to appear within fifty days at the tribunal of Heaven to answer for his murder. The menace was realised. Duke Francis died within the appointed time, struck with remorse, and terrified at the summons of the Cordelier. The monk was never seen again. On the death of Gilles, the Duke of Brittany himself wished to marry Françoise, but she would not listen to his proposals; and at last was obliged, in order to recover her liberty, to marry the aged Comte de Laval, father of her betrothed, with whom she lived peacefully thirty years, and had three sons. Duke Francis II. appointed her to the charge of rearing his daughter Anne.

Arthur Montauban turned monk to avoid the vengeance of Duke Peter, brother of Gilles, and eventually became Archbishop of Bordeaux. The Pope gave him the Abbey of Rédon, but popular indignation prevented him from accepting the appointment.

On our return from Montafilant we stopped to visit the Lunatic Asylum (Asile des aliénés), called Les Bas Foins, kept by the brothers of Saint-Jean-de-Dieu. There are six hundred inmates under the charge of about sixty brethren. The buildings, with the chapel, are very handsome and most complete in all the arrangements. Within the enclosure is a large piece of land. The lunatics are employed in agricultural, garden, and house occupations; they look very contented and happy. Visitors are not allowed to speak to them. We omitted seeing the Croix du Saint Esprit, a curiously sculptured Gothic granite cross of the fourteenth century, not far from the asylum.

The castle of Dinan is now a prison. It was occupied by the Queen-Duchess Anne, when on her way to a pilgrimage to Notre Dame-du-Folgoët, in fulfilment of a vow made during the illness of Louis XII. In the chapel is shewn a sculptured seat, still called the arm-chair of the Duchess Anne. Within these walls were crammed, in the last century, about 2000 English prisoners of war, many of whom fell victims to a contagious fever. From the platform of the keep we had a magnificent view of the surrounding country, extending to Mont Dol and the sea.

The church of St. Sauveur has a richly sculptured Romanesque portal. It contains the heart of

Du Guesclin, transferred from the church of the Dominicans, where he desired it to be interred by the side of his wife Tiphaine. His body was buried at St. Denis, in a tomb King Charles V. caused to be made in his lifetime, and he left orders that on his death his Constable should repose at his feet. On the dark-coloured monumental stone now incrusted on the wall, are roughly sculptured his arms (an eagle displayed charged with a cotice,[1]), with a commemorative inscription in gold letters:—

> "Cy: gist: le cueur: de
> Missire: bertram: du gueaquī
> en: son vivāt: conētiable de
> france: qui: trepassa: le: xiii^e
> jour: de: jullet: l'an: mil iii^e
> IIII^{xx} dont: son: corps: repos
> avecques: ceulx: des: Roys
> a sainct: denis en France."

Above hangs a painting representing the Governor of Châteauneuf Randon, laying the keys of the town upon the dead body of the Constable.[2]

---

[1] In heraldic language, "argent, à l'aigle de sable éployée à deux têtes, becquée et membrée de gueules, à la cotice de gueules mise en bande, brochant sur le tout, ce qui semble être une brisure de cadet."

[2] The Governor of Châteauneuf Randon (Dép. Lozère) had promised Du Guesclin he would surrender the place if relief did not arrive in fourteen days. The morning dawned, and no help had come. Du Guesclin lay dead, and the governor

Many of the streets of Dinan preserve the character of the Middle Ages, the houses upon columns forming a kind of porch or covered way; and most curious of all is the dirty, steep, narrow, winding street, called the Rue de Jerzual, a ravine extending from the top of the town, in one pitch, to the river's

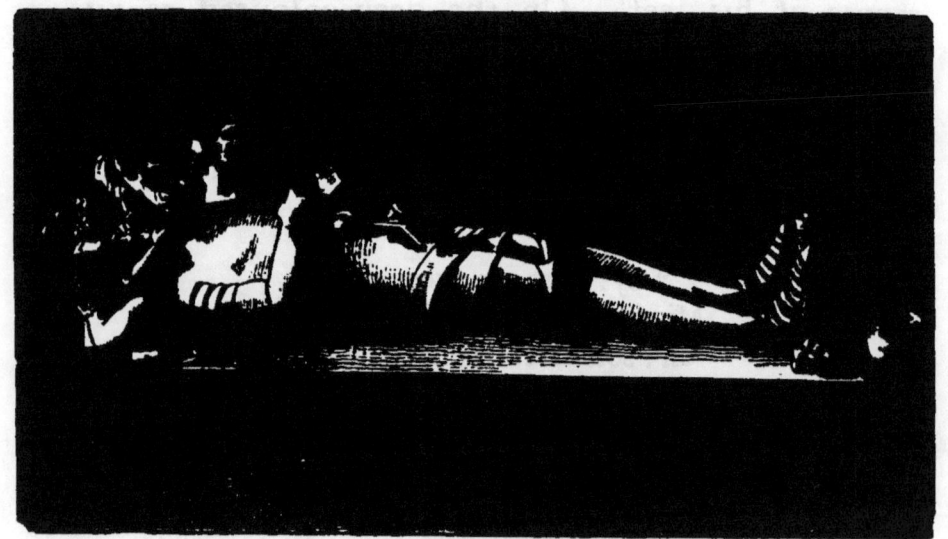

13.   Effigy of Jean de Beaumanoir.

edge. The Museum at the Mairie has an interesting collection of tumulary slabs—recumbent figures

refused to give up the keys to any but to him. At noontide, the gates of the city were thrown open, and the governor issued forth at the head of the garrison, traversed the army at the sound of trumpets, and entered the tent where the body of the dead hero lay, on a table covered with flowers, and surrounded by the chiefs of the army. The governor knelt beside the corpse, and reverently placed the keys on the coffin. "Thus," he said, "I fulfil my promise, and keep faith to thee, oh noble Du Guesclin, even in death."

taken from different churches and abbeys, mostly from the Beaumanoir chapel of the Abbey of Lehon. There is one of Jean de Beaumanoir, son of the hero of the "Combat des Trente," treacherously slain by his steward. He is represented in full armour, but with his head bare, to indicate the manner of his death. The effigy of his wife is also in complete armour, but on the belt that encircles her waist, like those worn by the knights, is sculptured a wreath of roses. She was a Du Guesclin by birth, and her feet repose upon an eagle, the bearing of her house. The statue of Roland, Vicomte de Dinan, one of the nine great Barons of Brittany in the twelfth century, is of gigantic proportions; the warrior is clad from head to foot in chain mail, but he holds one of his gauntlets in his hand. In the Museum is also a clock given to the city of Dinan by the Duchess Anne, inscribed with the name of its maker and the date of its construction: "1498, à Nantes par M. Hainzer de cette ville." The ancient bronze standard measures (étalons) of Dinan are decorated with the arms of the City, and Gothic inscriptions in relief, "Cart (quart) à gros blé pour Dinan"—"Cart à fourmant (froment) pour Dinan"—and "Bouesceau à scel (boisseau à sel) pour Dinan." Portraits of Du Guesclin and other Breton worthies are in one of the rooms (Salle de l'Odéon). That of the Constable answers to the description given of his appearance. He was low in stature, with large Breton head, broad shoulders, long arms, and large hands. His eyes were green, and his complexion swarthy: "la peau noire comme un sanglier."

14.   Château of La Bellière.

The drives round Dinan are endless in variety,[1] and all beautiful. We took a carriage to see the Château of la Bellière, about five miles and a half from Dinan, formerly the residence of Du Guesclin's

[1] "Tel est Dinan, la ville aux sites poétiques,
    Aux coteaux escarpés, aux vallons romantiques;
    Qui, gracieuse, élève, au milieu des vergers,
    Ses remparts tout couverts de jardins et d'ombrage,
    Son château crénelé, monument d'un autre age,
        Et les dômes de ses clochers."—AUBRY.

wife, the celebrated Lady Tiphaine; her name answers probably to our English Tiffany:—

> "William de Coningsby—
> Came out of Brittany
> With his wife Tiffany
> And her maid Manifas
> And his doggs Hardigras."

The Lady Tiphaine was heiress and daughter of the Vicomte de Bellière; so deeply versed was she in astrology, she was called Tiphaine la Fée. During her husband's absence in Spain, she resided at Mont Saint Michel, having chosen this insulated spot for the facilities it afforded her of studying the stars. She gave Du Guesclin a calendar on vellum, containing verses at the beginning of each month, pointing out the lucky and unlucky days; how many she marked down as such, we know not. Tycho Brahe had thirty-two fatal days in his calendar. Had Du Guesclin consulted this precious volume, which is now preserved in the Library at Avranches, he would never have risked his fortune by fighting the battle of Auray on the Feast of St. Michel, one of the fatal days against which she specially warns him in her book. We wished to have seen the room where she died, and where many memorials of her are preserved; but the proprietor was at his déjeuner, and would not grant us admittance, so we were forced to be content with seeing the exterior of the house, a château of the end of the fourteenth century. It stands on the edge of a large sheet of water, in the midst of trees on the roadside between Dinan and St. Malo. Its principal characteristics are its tall octagonal chimney-shafts, composed of granite, brick, and slate. They are surmounted by pieces of slate placed edgeways and forming a kind of capital or coronet to the granite shaft. Some of the chimneys have two circles of these coronets, and others are enriched with little rows of arches, of which the sombre slate background throws out the delicate ornamentation. Recrossing the magnificent viaduct, we proceeded to visit the Benedictine Priory of Lehon, called in the country "Chapelle des Beaumanoirs" from the mortuary chapel of that family attached to the abbey:—

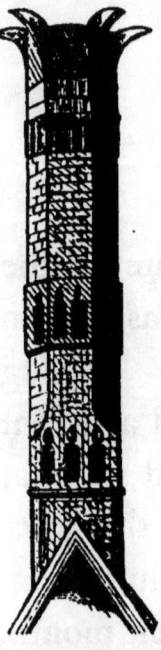

15. Chimney. Château of La Bellière.

> "Beaumanoir! à ce nom de glorieux prodiges
> Des siècles écoulés réveillent les prestiges:
> La pierre des tombeaux a paru se mouvoir
> Et des trente Bretons les clameurs belliqueuses
> Semblent répondre, sous ces voûtes fameuses,
> A ce grand nom de Beaumanoir."—AUBRY.

The west front, with its round-arched portal surmounted by a large Gothic window, is very pretty. The chapel of the Beaumanoirs was ravaged at the Revolution, the lead of the coffins sold, and the bones scattered. The statues have since been removed to the Museum at Dinan, and the crypt beneath, where they were buried, is inaccessible. At the Revolution, when the monks were expelled, the priory was sold and used for a spinning factory; and the weight of the machines crushed the floors, so as to shut up the entrance to the vaults. In the parish church adjacent, is to be noticed an ancient baptismal font, of cylindrical form, sculptured within and without. We returned home by the Château du Chêne-Ferron, approached by an avenue of firs, and had a lovely drive along the banks of the Rance.

Our last excursion in Dinan was to the Château of La Garaye, rendered famous by the virtues and boundless charity of its last proprietors, Count Claude Toussaint Marot de la Garaye and his wife, whose interesting story is told in the charming poem of Mrs. Norton:—

> "Listen to the tale I tell,
> Grave the story is—not sad;
> And the peasant plodding by
> Greets the place with kindly eye,
> For the inmates that it had."
>
> THE LADY OF LA GARAYE.

Count Claude de la Garaye and his wife were young, beautiful, and endowed with friends, riches, and all that could make life bright and happy. They entertained with hospitality, and enjoyed the pleasures and amusements of the world; when one day the Countess was thrown from her horse, the expectations of an heir vanished, and she was left a cripple for life. Both were inconsolable for their disappointment. One day a monk came to visit them, and tried to comfort them, seeking by his converse to turn their thoughts from earthly affections to heavenly consolation—

"Ah! my father," said the lady, "how happy are you, to love nothing on earth!"

"You are mistaken," answered the monk; "I love all those who are in sorrow or suffering, and I submit myself to the will of the Almighty, and bend myself with resignation to every blow He strikes."

He proceeded to show them there was still great happiness in store for them, in ministering to the comforts of others. Following his counsel, they went to Paris; for three years the Count studied medicine and surgery, and his wife became a skilful oculist. On their return to La Garaye, they gave up all the amusements of society, and devoted themselves to relieving the sufferings of their fellow creatures. Their house was converted into an hospital for the sick and the wounded, under the ministering care of the Count and his benevolent wife:—

"Her home is made their home; her wealth their dole;
Her busy courtyard hears no more the roll
Of gilded vehicles, or pawing steeds,
But feeble steps of those whose bitter needs
Are their sole passport. Through that gateway pass
All varying forms of sickness and distress,
And many a poor worn face that hath not smiled
For years,—and many a feeble crippled child,—
Blesses the tall, white portal where they stand,
And the dear Lady of the liberal hand."

THE LADY OF LA GARAYE.

Nor was their philanthropy confined to their own province. In 1720, they offered themselves to M. de Belzunce—"Marseilles' good bishop"—to assist him during the visitation of the Plague. The fame of their virtues reached even the French Court, and Louis XV. sent Count de la Garaye the order of St. Lazarus with a donation of 50,000 livres and a contract on the post of 25,000 more.

They both died at an advanced age, within two years of each other, and were buried among their poor at Taden, but their marble mausoleum in the church was destroyed in the French Revolution. Count de la Garaye[1] left a large sum to be distributed among the prisoners, principally English, at Rennes and Dinan, who were suffering pent up in these crowded gaols. The Comte had attended the English prisoners at Dinan during a contagious

---

[1] Count Claude died in 1755, at the age of eighty-one. The countess in 1757, at seventy-six.

fever, called the "peste blanche," and, in acknowledgment of his humanity, Queen Caroline sent him two dogs with silver collars round their necks, and an English nobleman made him a present of six more.

16.   Château of La Garaye.

The ruined château is approached by an ivy-covered gateway, through an avenue of beeches:—

> "Le lierre flottant comme un manteau de deuil,
> Couvre à demi la porte et rampe sur le seuil."
> <p align="right">LAMARTINE, <i>Harmonies Poëtiques.</i></p>

or, as Mrs. Norton renders it:—

> "And like a mourner's mantle, with sad grace,
> Waves the dark ivy—hiding half the door
> And threshold, where the weary traveller's foot
> Shall never find a courteous welcome more."

It is fast falling to pieces. The principal part remaining is an octagonal turret of three stories, with elegant Renaissance decoration round the windows. One more quotation from Mrs. Norton, and we quit these hallowed ruins:—

> "We know the healthy stir of human life
> Must be for ever gone!
> The walls where hung the warrior's shining casque
> Are green with moss and mould;
> The blindworm coils where Queens have slept, nor asks
> For shelter from the cold.
> The swallow,—he is master all the day,
> And the great owl is ruler through the night;
> The little bat wheels on his circling way,
> With restless flittering flight;
> And that small bat, and the creeping things,
> At will they come and go,
> And the soft white owl with velvet wings,
> And a shout of human woe!
> The brambles let no footsteps pass
> By that rent in the broken stair,
> When the pale tufts of the windle-strae grass
> Hang like locks of dry dead hair;
> But there the keen sound ever sweeps and moans,
> Working a passage through the mouldering stones."
>
> THE LADY OF LA GARAYE.

From Dinan, instead of taking the customary road to the railway station of Caulnes, we hired a carriage, in order to visit the fortress castle of La Hunaudaye, midway between Dinan and Lamballe. The road lay by Jugon, a town prettily situated in the cleft of two hills. On one once stood an important castle, which gave rise to the saying:—

> "Qui a Bretagne sans Jugon,
> A chape sans chaperon."

Jugon is on the edge of two ponds. One of them, the largest in Brittany, hangs suspended over the town, as if threatening it with inundation. They told us it was swarming with fish of every description, and with pike of fabulous dimensions. Turning off the road to the right, we entered the forest of La Hunaudaye, and walked in a pouring rain to the château, situated a short distance from the road. It is of vast extent, has five round towers with ramparts of cut stone, and is surrounded by walls with machicolated parapets. It is a splendid ruin, but the incessant rain prevented us from spending much time in its examination. It was built in the thirteenth century by Olivier de la Tournemine, and was one of the strongest fortresses in Brittany. Situated in the midst of a vast forest, its lord and his retainers were the terror of the surrounding country. No traveller passed untaxed; all were compelled to pay toll. In 1504, the Bishop of St. Brieuc complains to the Parliament at Rennes that, regardless of the safeguard of the Duke, the foresters of the Lord of La Hunaudaye had carried off his horses, trunks, and baggage, and, a year later, they had the audacity to stop the Queen-

Duchess Anne on her way to a pilgrimage to the Folgoët. The Queen was conducted to the presence of the Lord of La Hunaudaye, who maintained to her that he had only exercised his right of exacting a ransom from all who passed through the forest without his permission, but that he waived his privilege in favour of his Sovereign. Be that as it may, he received her Majesty most royally, as the old chaplain, Oliver de la Roche recounts, and gave a splendid banquet, which he fully describes. The table, he says, was four times covered with thirty-six dishes of viands, and lastly, was brought in, "en grande vénération," by eight squires, a whole calf, standing on its legs, well seasoned, with an orange in its mouth; and, when it appeared, the trumpets sounded so loud that it seemed as if the walls shook. On seeing the "dainty dish" that was "set before the Queen," all wished to have a share; and the chaplain relates, with great satisfaction, how he was served himself twice by the Lord of La Hunaudaye.

The dark deeds of the lords of La Hunaudaye have given rise to many a legend. The following is a translation of one of the most popular:—

LEGEND OF LA HUNAUDAYE.
(*Translation.*)

"When the rock eagle wakes,
And the towers of Hunaudaye
Gleam like three phantom forms
In the morning's sunlight ray;

When night her darksome wing
Folds round this desert waste,
Shun all this cursed ground—
Traveller flee thou in haste.

"There once—Great Heaven shield
Us all! and no ill arise—
There once—Hush! leave me not;
Hear you, from the ground, low sighs?—
There once—wrapped in the gloom
Of a dark and rainy night,
A man of haughty mien
Knocked at the door of might.

"'Open!' cried he,—it turns
On groaning hinge. The rain
Pours, but the frightened guards
Mark neither spot nor stain
On his purple cloak—nor his plumes
Droop wet, yet the torrents fall
Wildly and fast to night,
Beating the castle wall.

"The baron, stern and sad,
Was in his tower alone,
Pacing, with mailed heel,
Upon the echoing stone:
Cried he—'What stranger seeks,
This hour, my castle drear?
Ho! Oliver, Ho! Ralph,
See who intrudeth here.'

"'Heaven shield thee, baron brave!
A strange knight in the hall
Craves audience.' 'Lead him here:
Stay thou and Ralph in call,
At need.' Silent and slow
The purple-mantled knight,
Advancing, paused—his looks
Gleaming unearthly bright.

"'Who art thou coming thus,
　Loud clamouring at my gate,
　Thou truly puissant knight,
　With not one squire for state?
　Knowst thou at word of mine ——'
　The stranger knight smiled stern,
　Replied in awful voice,
'Would'st thou my name? now learn:
　Here is my train—behold!'
　He cried.　There hideous stood
　One spectre, then two more—
　A sight to chill the blood—
　Unveiled their features pale,
　All three in cere-cloth dressed,
　Opening all wide to point
　Where blood flowed from the breast.

"'Baron, these are my guard,'
　Said the unknown—'Here, lo!
　Thy father's aged form,
　By poignard stroke laid low;
　Here thy wife, cruelly slain
　In the year thy brother fell;
　They stand, pale, bleeding, stiff,—
　Their murderer, can'st thou tell?'

"The phantoms three enlaced
　The trembling baron round;
　He vainly shrieked,—the walls
　With demon laughs resound;
　The echoing thunders rolled
　Along the valley deep;
　Lightnings, when pale dawn broke,
　Blasted the castle keep.

"It stands a blackened pile;
　The ruined gate is there.
　But the sky lowers dark,
　Oh! traveller flee, beware;

F

> At this hour the shades of night
> Brood o'er the solemn gloom.
> Traveller, haste, oh! haste;
> Leave this abode of doom."

It was in the forest of La Hunaudaye that the Chouans of the Côtes du Nord were secretly exercised and drilled by their chief, La Rouërie, under the name of Gosselin, who died of horror on hearing of the execution of thirteen of his confederates betrayed by the physician Chaftal. Gosselin was succeeded by the "Cid" of the Chouan chiefs, Boishardy, called the "Sorcier," who, after his interview with General Humbert, was betrayed and shot by the "Bleus." For twelve years was Brittany cut off from France by this Chouan war, an insurrection even more formidable than that of La Vendée. The peninsular position of Brittany, its vast extent of coasts, its forests, its mountains, its people, speaking a strange language, entirely under the subjection of the priests, rendered it peculiarly adapted to carry on a war against the republicans; a war, the whole object of which was to upset all order, by preventing the citizens from accepting office under the republic, by punishing those who acquired national property, by stopping couriers and all public conveyances, destroying bridges, breaking up roads, assassinating public officers, and executing horrible punishments on those who sent provisions into the towns.

The castle of La Hunaudaye was destroyed by order of the Commune of Lamballe, in 1793, that it might not serve as a retreat for the Chouans.

We arrived very wet at Lamballe, a town most picturesquely situated on the declivity of a granite cliff, surmounted by a handsome church, rising from the very edge of the rocks. It formed part of the territory of the Duke of Penthièvre, whose heiress, Jeanne la Boiteuse, married Charles of Blois, the competitor with John de Montfort[1] for the dukedom

---

[1] It may appear almost superfluous to refer to the cause of the War of Succession, which for twenty years devastated Brittany, and brought the armies of France and England into the duchy. John III. died in 1341, leaving no children. He had a brother Guy, Comte de Penthièvre, and a half-brother, John de Montfort. Charles left the succession to Charles de Châtillon, Comte de Blois, nephew of Philip Augustus, King of France, who had married Jeanne, the only daughter and heiress of Guy; but his half-brother, John de Montfort, seized the duchy. The decision was referred to the King of France, who gave it in favour of his relation Charles of Blois. De Montfort sought the protection of the King of England, whom he acknowledged as King of France, and Edward III. readily gave him his support. It became no longer the dispute of a province, but of two mighty nations, in which the Kings of France, England, and Navarre took part, and which was illustrated by the names of Chandos, Manny, Du Guesclin and Clisson. The Bretons on the east of the province sided with the French prince, those of the promontory with the son of de Montfort. The battle of Auray, 1364, decided the war in favour of De Montfort, but the contest did not finally cease till the marriage of Anne de Bretagne to Charles VIII. united the duchy to the French crown.

of Brittany. More tenacious of her rights than her husband, Jeanne would never listen to any compromise. After the treaty of Bretigny, the kings of England and France proposed a division of the duchy between the two rivals; but, intimidated by his wife, Charles dared not consent; and again, before the battle of Auray, when a division was agreed upon, subject to the acceptance of the Countess, Jeanne exclaimed, " My husband makes too cheap a bargain of what is not his own." And she wrote to Charles, " Do what you please. I am a woman, and cannot do more; but I had rather lose my life, or two if I had them, before I would consent to so reproachable an act, to the shame of my family" (*des miens*). Later she said to him, "Preserve me your heart, but preserve me also my duchy, and, happen what may, act so that the sovereignty remains to me entire." Her pride and obstinacy cost her husband his life. The name of Lamballe is associated with the memory of the unfortunate Princesse de Savoie de Carignan, the sad victim of revolutionary fury. On the death of her husband, the Prince de Lamballe, the vast estates of the Penthièvre family passed to his sister, the wife of Philippe Egalité, and from her descended to Louis Philippe, King of the French.

Next day we made an excursion to the famed Temple of Lanleff, in Breton, the " land of tears," situated in a retired valley about six miles from the sea. According to the tradition of the country, it was built by "Les moines rouges," as they style the Templar Knights. The road was incessantly up and down hill, as we afterwards found they are throughout Brittany; a " pays accidenté" it may be truly called. The chapel of Lanleff is composed of two concentric circular enclosures separated by

17.   Section of Lanleff Church.

twelve round arches, with cushion-shaped capitals, having heads, human and animal, rudely sculptured upon them at the four angles. Its whole diameter is about twenty-two feet. It was probably built by some Templar Knight in the beginning of the twelfth century on his return from the Holy Land. The number of arches may allude to that of the twelve Apostles.

The parish church was built into the east side of the temple, the only part which has preserved its roof, and which served as a vestibule to the more modern building. A gigantic yew formerly grew in the central enclosure, and overshadowed it with its spreading branches; but the parish church has been taken down and rebuilt in another part of the village, and the yew-tree has disappeared.

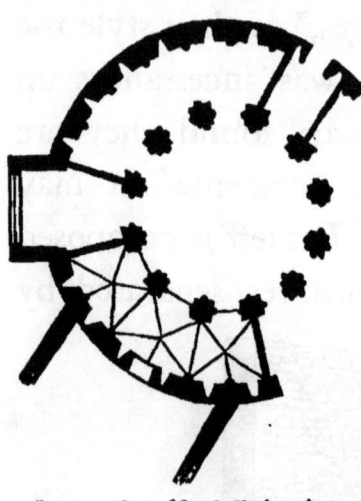

18.   Plan of Lanleff Church.

Close to the temple is a spring enclosed by flag-stones. When moistened, they appear covered with blood-stained spots. According to the tradition, in olden times an unnatural father sold his child to the Evil One. The gold received for the bargain was counted out upon the side of the spring, and the accursed money left its print upon the stones. A bare-legged peasant who stood by with her pitcher, threw some water over the stones, and immediately there appeared round red spots of different sizes— indelible marks of the diabolical bargain. We went into a cottage close by, and had some boiled eggs and cider. The inmates were at their meal—a bowl of milk, into which they broke their buckwheat "galette." We were much struck with the jealous pertinacity of the Breton, to show he considers himself as of a different people and country to the rest of France, a feeling which more than three hundred years has not dissipated. Our driver would talk of Bretons and French as of distinct nations, and the Normans in this part of Brittany are the special objects of hatred, originating, perhaps, in the former subjection of Brittany to Normandy. When Charles the Simple ceded to the fierce Northmen the province now known by their name, their sovereignty extended over Brittany, and the dukes of Normandy did homage for both provinces to the King of France. The Bretons struggled hard against the supremacy of the Barbarians, but eventually had to acknowledge the Duke of Normandy as their sovereign lord.

St. Brieuc, principal town of the department of the Côtes-du-Nord, has been described as an old town with a new face. Though one of the oldest in Brittany, it has little of antiquity to detain the traveller. The Palais de Justice is a handsome building, in the midst of a pretty garden, commanding a view of the Tour de Cesson, lower down the river (the Gouët), a large circular tower built by Duke John IV., and blown up by Henry IV., at the desire of the Briochins, as the inhabitants of St. Brieuc style themselves. The mine split it in two, and the part that remains serves as a landmark for the pilots between St. Brieuc and its port, about two miles distant, called Légué. Notre Dame d'Espérance is a pretty church, rebuilt about ten years since, with a calvary in front, and a series of painted windows representing the principal saints of Brittany, and the most celebrated pilgrimages of the Virgin in that province. At St. Brieuc, 1689, James II. of England reviewed his little army, and was received with royal honours by the bishop of the place.

We proceeded by the railway to Guingamp, next to St. Brieuc, the principal town of the department, capital of the duchy of Penthièvre. It is situated in the richly wooded and cultivated valley of the Trieux, a favourite fishing river of considerable size, and affording trout, salmon, and dace, from Guingamp to Paimpol, where it falls into the sea, a distance of twenty miles. It runs through the centre of the town, and is here a considerable stream.

Attached to the Cathedral is the venerated sanctuary of Notre Dame-du-Bon-Secours, one of the most celebrated places of pilgrimage in Brittany. The pardon takes place the Saturday before the first Sunday in July, and owes its origin to the brotherhood called the "Frérie blanche," an association of which Duke Peter accepted the title of lay-abbot. The motto embroidered on their banner was (in Breton) "A triple cord is not easily broken." The triple cord being emblematic of the three estates—clergy, nobles, and laity—in whose unity consisted the strength of Brittany. The Frérie blanche no

19.   Fountain of Duke Peter.

longer exists, the triple cable is broken, the pilgrimage alone remains.

La Pompe, or the fountain of Duke Peter, as it is

called, is of later dater date, being in the style of the Renaissance. It consists of three circular basins in tiers. On the lower are sea-horses, which, with their wings, support the second basin, and Naiads uphold the third. On the top is a figure of the Virgin with her arms extended.

The women of Guingamp wear high muslin caps, dark petticoats, and black stockings. Knitting-pins in hand, they work away at their stockings whether walking, talking, or with a load of butter on their heads, as they do throughout all Brittany. When not at work, their knitting-pins are stuck in their hair. Knitting and spinning are the occupation of their lives. When the Breton's idol, Du Guesclin, was a prisoner to the Black Prince, and was asked how he could raise the large sum named for his ransom, Du Guesclin replied, that "the women of Brittany would rather spin for a year and ransom him with their distaffs, than that he should remain prisoner."

> " Quand vous étiez captif, Bertrand, fils de Bretagne,
> Tous les fuseaux tournaient aussi dans la campagne ;
> Chaque femme apporte son écheveau de lin ;
> Ce fut votre rançon, messire Du Guesclin !"
>
> *Les Bretons*, A. BRIZEUX.

Guingamp was given by Duke John V. to his son Peter, who resided here and rebuilt the castle. When attacked by his mortal illness, the physicians attributed his malady to witchcraft, and declared it could only be remedied by counter-spells. The Prince refused to have recourse to such means, saying, "I had rather die by the will of God, than live by the will of the Devil."—"J'aime mieux mourir de par Dieu, que de vivre de par le Diable."

We walked to the small chapel of St. Léonard, picturesquely situated on a little eminence. It was built by Charles of Blois, on his return from his captivity in England, and dedicated by him to St. Léonard, the patron-saint of prisoners—a contemporary of Clovis, from whom he obtained permission to set free all the captives he should find in the prisons. In the month of May, people who are attacked with fever repair to St. Léonard to seek, upon the walls of the chapel or on the calvary attached to it, snails as cures for their malady. They must gather them themselves, pound them, and put them into little bags, which they wear round their necks. As soon as the fever leaves them they bury their bags at the foot of the walls of the chapel, and, if they fail to perform this ceremony, the fever will return. We found quantities of these bags, made of coarse linen, lying half-buried under the walls of the chapel. There is a pardon here every year, on which occasion only the chapel is opened.

We took a carriage to Paimpol. On our way we stopped at the Château de Boisgelin, belonging to the Marquis of the same name, but could not obtain admittance. On to the Abbey of Beauport (Sancta Maria de Bello Porto), founded in the thirteenth century, beautifully situated on a tongue of land at the entrance of the Bay of Paimpol, opposite the island of Saint-Rion. In its large garden, which extends down to the sea, are planted myrtles, figs, mulberries, and other trees of the south of Europe. Beauport has been called the Chartreuse of Brittany. It is a lovely secluded spot, as, indeed, are most of the sites of the old abbeys, varying in aspect, but always beautiful. No description can give an idea of the magnificent panoramic views from the walls of the abbey.

M. Merimée justly observes, " It appears strange that, in so early a stage of civilisation, the monks should be so alive to the beauties of nature. The contemplative habits of monastic life must at all times have imparted to the mind a feeling of abstract beauty, independent of any idea of real utility. Secure of an uniform, peaceful existence, limited in his pleasures and his ambition, sheltered by his sacred office, above others, from the reverses of fortune, the monk of the thirteenth century was in a position to love, and did love, beauty for itself. And while the knight, at war with all the world, thought only on building an impregnable fortress, the abbot embellished his dwelling, and tasted the enjoyments afforded by imagination and the arts. "The abbey

Abbey of Beauport.

of Beauport is built in the pointed style, and is a perfect example of the monastic architecture of the thirteenth century—the most important and most beautiful convent ruins in Brittany. The original disposition of its buildings may yet be clearly traced. These abbeys were all built upon the same plan. In the centre was the square garden (préau), surrounded by the cloisters. On the south side the church, extending from west to east; on the north, the refectory, with the kitchen attached. On the east was the chapter-house, and some small apartments; above these were the dormitories. Outside was the interior court, reserved for the brethren, and beyond, the great court, into which the provisions were brought, and round which were the stables and farm buildings. The garden, orchard, mill, oven, dovecote, cider-press, &c., were all within the walled enclosure, for the abbeys were not merely convents dedicated solely to devotional exercises. After prayer followed labour. The Breton abbeys were quite model farms; the woods and the commons afforded the means of rearing cattle to those who had the privilege of pasturage in the forests. Many had also the right of acorns and beech-mast for their pigs (*droit au gland et à la faîne*). One abbey, that of Morimond (Haute Marne), is recorded to have had twenty piggeries, of three hundred pigs each, distributed in its forests. The monks also reared sheep and horses, and fattened fish in their ponds. They were the first who advanced the science of horticulture and the cultivation of vegetables. To these agricultural pursuits were added, in many convents, the industrial arts, and some of the brethren were brewers, curriers, fullers, weavers, shoemakers, carpenters, and blacksmiths. Their cultivation of the liberal arts and sciences is well known. During the Middle Ages the monasteries were the sole depositories of learning. Beauport is now occupied by a Polish lady, Countess Poninsky, who allows no one to enter the abbey, as her husband was buried in the church.

Two or three miles further we reached Paimpol, where we remained the night, at a nice hotel. Paimpol is a seaport town prettily situated in a cultivated country on the bay that bears its name. Its inhabitants are employed in the mackerel and Iceland fisheries. The women about here wear close straw-bonnets. They all, in this department, ride on horseback, "à califourchon," like the men.

We hired our carriage on to Tréguier. At Lézardrieux we passed the estuary of the Trieux, over a magnificent suspension-bridge, at a considerable elevation above the water, vessels sail under it. It was built 1840, and is 833 feet long, that is, 167 longer than the famed bridge of La Roche Bernard (Loire Inférieure). The bridge swung frightfully when we passed over it. In the churchyard of Pleudaniel is a pretty granite calvary, and skulls are placed in recesses in the wall on each side of the church-porch.

We next came to the Château of La Roche Jagu, on the summit of a hill overhanging the river Trieux and defending the entrance. It has more of the character of a "maison forte" than of a "manoir," as was termed the habitation of a knight, and of those who holding a fief, yet did not possess the seignorial right to a castle with towers and donjon. The manoir might be enclosed by walls and moats, but not with towers. The entrance on the side opposite to the river is through a large walled court by a low Gothic doorway, closed by an enormous iron grating of upright and horizontal bars of great thickness, hanging on four hinges, and secured by four locks; all the windows have gratings of the same kind. A stone staircase leads to the one story, consisting of a suite of large rooms half lighted by narrow windows. Some of these are occupied by the keeper of the castle and others are reserved for the use of the proprietor, the Marquis d'Argentré, and, when he goes there, are decorated and partly furnished with the pieces of old tapestry lying about. At the end of these rooms is a turret, which communicates with a covered gallery surmounting the whole length of the façade facing the river, and commanding a beautiful view of the windings of the silvery Trieux and of its fir-clothed banks. This gallery is furnished with battlements, and served the double purpose of a rampart and an observatory. The wall on the river-side is fifteen feet thick, and a chapel hewn in the thickness of the wall is lighted by a Gothic window looking over the Trieux. Fourteen elegant chimney-shafts of cut stone, cylindrical in form, and ornamented with iron spikes, give a most original character to the building. The château belonged to the Maréchal Duc de Richelieu, who sold it in 1773 to the Tressan family, under the stipulation that its subterranean passages should not be explored. They are said to extend under the bed of the river to the Château of Frinandour, half a league distant.

We next passed through Pontrieux, a pretty, small town, seated in a deep valley, the river Trieux flowing through it. The river here is famous for salmon, and there is a considerable commerce in its little port.

La Roche Derrien on the Jaudy, during the War of Succession in Brittany, was a castle of some celebrity. It was here Charles of Blois was taken prisoner by the English, who, under Sir Thomas Dagworth, were in possession of the place. Charles of Blois assembled a large army, and attacked them by night. Three times was he rescued, and three times retaken; he had received eighteen wounds, and was at last compelled to surrender. Jeanne de Montfort, like all women who hate, was very vindictive, and caused her illustrious prisoner to be ignominiously dragged to Quimperlé, Vannes, and Hennebont, whence he was transferred to London, and confined in the Tower. It was nine years before he regained his liberty. Meanwhile his heroic wife, Jeanne de Penthièvre, became head of his party, as Jeanne de Flandre was that of the De Montfort. The "War of the two Jeannes" continued for nine years, during which they fought with fierceness and courage, and ruled with ability. Curious,—the history of France was illustrated in this century by five heroines of the name of Jeanne: Jeanne d'Arc, Jeanne Hachette of Beauvais, and the Jeannes of Penthièvre, Flandre, and Clisson, who made themselves famous in Brittany. On his release, Charles of Blois gave La Roche-Derrien to Du Guesclin. The castle was demolished, but a calvary has been built on the site.

Not far from La Roche-Derrien is the church of Langoat, which contains the monument of Ste. Pompée (1370), mother of St. Tugdual. On the granite tomb reposes her marble effigy, and around it bas-reliefs in Gothic niches represent the life of the saint. In all the churches in this district, tressels are placed in the nave ready for funerals. The gravestones have in each a little hollow well, to contain water for sprinkling over the grave, or in some a small basin is set upon the gravestone, with a sprig of box laid by the side, for the same pious purpose.

Every one must be struck by the excellence of the roads in Brittany, as indeed throughout France; in no instance does the French administrative talent more fully display itself. The roads are of three classes: the "routes impériales," under the care of the Government; "départementales," kept entirely at the expense of the department; and the "chemins vicinaux," which belong to the communes or parishes, and which all the inhabitants are called upon to support. To each lieue de poste (two and a half miles), is appointed a "cantonnier" or road-keeper, who is responsible for the condition of the length of road assigned to his care.

We stopped at Kermartin, a farmhouse near Tréguier, to see the bed said to have belonged to St. Ives, the favourite saint of the Bretons, and whose name is borne by the majority of the inhabitants of the district of Tréguier and St. Brieuc. Charles of Blois held him in great veneration. He gave part of a rib of St. Ives to the church at Lamballe, and carried the relic in procession barefooted to the church. Before the battle of Auray, he ordered his men to march "in the name of God and St. Yves."

St. Ives, or Yves Hélory, was one of the most remarkable characters of the thirteenth century. He studied law in the schools of Paris, and applied his talents in defending the cause of the poor; hence he was called "the poor man's advocate;" and so great to this day is the confidence placed in his justice, that, in the department of the Côtes-du-Nord, when a debtor falsely denies his debt, a peasant will pay twenty sous for a mass to St. Yves, convinced that St. Yves will cause the faithless creditor to die within the year. His truthfulness was such, he was called St. Yves de Verité. He is the special patron of lawyers, and always represented in the "mortier," or lawyer's cap, with an ermine-trimmed scarlet robe.

> "Saint Yves était Breton,
> Avocat et pas larron,
> Chose rare, se dit-on."

Lawyers, says a writer, take him for a patron, but not for a model. Philip le Hardi, in acknowledgment of his worth, granted him a pension of six deniers a day—in those times a considerable sum.

Over this house is a marble tablet with this inscription:—

"Ici est né le 17 Octr 1253, et est mort le 19 Mai 1303,

SAINT YVES,

Officiel de Tréguier, curé de Tredretz et de Lohannec. Sa maison, qui a subsisté jusqu'en l'année 1834, ayant été alors demolie à cause de vetusté, Mg^r Hyacinthe Louis de Quelen, Arch^rque de Paris, et propriétaire des domaines de Kermartin, a fait placer cette inscription, afin qu'un lieu sanctifié par la presence d'un si grand serviteur de Dieu ne demeurât pas inconnu (1837)."

The house is a good specimen of a Breton dwelling; by the side of the fire, in the one room of which most of these cottages consist, fixed against the wall like the berth of a ship, stands the bedstead or "lit clos" of old oak, shut in by carved and well-waxed sliding panels, often inscribed with the sacred monogram. The two mattresses, paillasse, and "cossette de plume," are piled up to such a height as barely to admit of its tenants creeping into the bed. In front is the customary chest, containing the family wardrobe, answering the double purpose of a seat and the means of ascending into the bed. Often we have seen cupboards on each side of the large chimney with two shelves, which served as beds for the juvenile members of the family. Forms and a polished table complete the furniture; the last has frequently little wells hollowed in the top, used, instead of plates, to hold the soup. Over the table, suspended by pulleys, are two indispensable articles in a Breton dwelling—a large circular basket to cover the bread, and a kind of wooden frame or rack, round which the spoons are ranged. Forks they do not use. Festoons of sausages, with hams, bacon, candles, skins of lard, onions, horse-shoes, harness, all hang suspended from the ceiling, which consists of fagots of hazel suspended by cross-poles. The floor is of beaten earth. One narrow window admits the light, and there are no outhouses. The manure-heap is generally at the house-door, and the pigs and poultry seem on an equally intimate footing as they are in our Irish cabins. The Breton's cottage has often no garden, to occupy his leisure hours; and the men, after their daily work, resort to the cabaret to spend their time and their earnings. Agriculture is very backward in Brittany, but the land produces abundance of corn. It is thrashed out direct from the field, on a clay floor (aire). Beet-root and clover grow very luxuriantly, and in some fields the pretty red clover (*Trifolium incarnatum*) carpets the country with its crimson flowers.

Near the farmhouse of Kermartin is the parish church of Minihy-Tréguier, formerly a chapel founded by St. Ives and attached to the "manoir." The will of St. Ives is framed and hung up in the church, and his breviary is also preserved here; but the guide said it was now kept at the priest's house, as people were in the habit of taking away a leaf as a relic. Minihy, *i.e.* Monk's House, is a name given to those places which, through the intercession of some saint, had the right of sanctuary. They were marked with a red cross, and, how great soever the crime, were regarded as inviolable. In 1441 the right of sanctuary was restricted to churches; before, it was extended to towns and districts. Tréguier had the privilege within a radius of twelve miles from the town. St. Malo also possessed the right of sanctuary. Tréguier is one of the four bishoprics that formed the ancient divisions of Brittany. The others were Léon, Cornouaille, and Vannes. The "pays de Tréguier" answers exactly to the present department of the Côtes-du-Nord; Léon to the territory or arrondissement of Brest and Morlaix; Cornouaille has Quimper and Carhaix for its principal towns; and Vannes, the country of Celtic remains, is to the south.

Tréguier is prettily situated on a hill, at the confluence of the rivers Jaudy and Guindy; its principal building is the beautiful, imposing cathedral, with its elegant spire, begun in the thirteenth century by St. Yves, and dedicated to St. Tugdual, whose name, like St. Yves, is often given in baptism to the Breton children. St. Yves is buried here, and also Duke John V., who founded the Chapelle du Duc, and desired to be interred at the feet of St. Yves, for whom he had a special regard, and to whom he erected a magnificent tomb, for three centuries the object of veneration in Brittany. The Duke paid for it his own weight in silver (389 marks 7 oz.), in 1424, to Maistre Jacques de Hougue. The victories of his father John the Conqueror were chased in bas-relief round the tomb, which was destroyed in 1793. Duke John V. was a contemptible prince, who eight times changed his party from weakness rather than policy, and on whom Margaret de Clisson and her sons retaliated the cowardly seizure of her father, the Constable Clisson, by Duke John IV. One of the towers of the cathedral is called the tower of Hastings, but its date is evidently subsequent to that of the Norman freebooter. The cathedral has preserved its beautiful cloisters, the work of the fifteenth century, although it has been ravaged by the Normans of the ninth century, the English in the fourteenth, the Spaniards in the sixteenth, and by the Revolutionists of 1793. It was the port chosen by the Constable Clisson, 1387, for the invasion of England, an expedition proposed and projected by himself. His hatred against the English was so great, though educated in England, he was termed the "boucher des Anglais." When the Duke of Brittany gave Chandos the château of Gavre, which was within a league of Clisson's château of Blain (Loire Inférieure), "I will never," he exclaimed, "be the neighbour of the English," and accordingly he sallied out one morning and burnt the castle to the ground. Chandos complained to the Black Prince, who sent a letter of remonstrance to Clisson, but it was only replied by a challenge to the Prince to meet him in single combat. Clisson caused his own ship to be built at Tréguier, and had constructed a tower or framework of large timber, to be put together on his landing in England, for the lords to retreat to as a place of safety, and to be lodged therein securely in the event of a night attack. This tower, Froissart says, was so constructed, that when dislodged it could be taken to pieces, and many carpenters and other workmen were engaged, at very high wages, to go with it to England to superintend the putting of it together. Four thousand men-at-arms and 2000 cross-bowmen were in readiness for the expedition, with horses, vessels laden with wine, salted provisions, and other necessaries. All these formidable preparations were rendered useless by the arrest of the Constable the day before his embarkation. We went to the Cemetery, which has its ossuary, reliquary, or bone-house, an inseparable appendage to a Breton churchyard. It is the custom in Brittany, after a certain time, to dig up the bones of the dead, and preserve their skulls in little square boxes, like dog-kennels, with a heart-shaped opening through which the skull is visible. They are all ticketed with the names and dates of the deceased, as "Ci gît le chef de * * * D. c. D. (décédé) le * * * * *. Priez Dieu pour son âme."

These boxes sometimes occupy prominent places inside the churches or porch, on window sills, the capitals of columns, and other ledges; but more often are ranged in the ossuaries or charnel-houses built in the churchyards to receive them, with a row of death's-heads carved in the stone outside.

21. Skull-box.

The large bones are also placed in the ossuaire. The rich are buried in "enfeux" or arched recesses in the chapels or abbeys they have founded.

We continued our carriage to Lannion, our driver not very clear of his way, and in Brittany the road is very difficult to be discerned; for on each side are high earthen banks, sometimes eight or ten feet high, and on the top of these are planted timber-trees, such as oak, elm, and ash, which often meet at the top, entirely intercepting the view, making these narrow lanes a perfect slough and most intricate to thread. Sometimes they are cut in irregular steps in the solid rock, and serve for the bed of a stream. Each field is also surrounded by these hedgerow-trees, which are cut every four or five years.

We drove to Perros Guirec, a lovely little watering-place built on a small promontory with a safe harbour, whence wheat, hemp, and cattle are exported to England; it is six miles from Lannion. A dangerous rock, called Roche Bernard, is at its entrance. The view is lovely. From Perros we scrambled over a hilly cart-road to Ploumanach, about three miles distant—a wonderful spot, huge round erratic blocks of pink granite flung over land and sea in the wildest confusion. The whole coast is one sea of boulders, a chaos of rocks of all sizes cover the soil in every direction, and in many places there is no soil at all, and the loose masses rest on a bare bed of rock, stretching, in unbroken extent, to a great distance. "A wanderer," says Mr. Trollope, "amid this strange and silent scene might fancy himself the only living thing in the midst of a world turned to stone. In every possible variety of uncouth form and capricious, strange positions, the endless masses were around us."

"All is rocks at random thrown,
  Black waves, bare crags, and banks of stone."
                                LORD OF THE ISLES.

One rock, surrounded at high water by the tide, is a square block of red granite of thirty to forty feet high, placed on the top of a still higher mass, on which it rests upon a very small base. It is called the "Roche Pendue," and serves as a landmark for the fishermen. We took a small boat full of fish resembling codlings or small cod, called "lieu," and were rowed by the fishermen through a sea of granite boulders to the opposite side of the Trégastel estuary, to see the "pierre pendue," or rocking-stone (Breton, *rouler*), the largest in Brittany. These stones are so nicely poised that they can be moved with the slighest impulse by any one knowing the exact point at which to touch them. They were used in early times as proving-stones, and called "Pierres de verité."

> "Firm as it seems,
> Such is its strange and virtuous property,
> It moves obsequious to the gentlest touch
> Of him whose breast is pure; but to a traitor,
> Though e'en a giant's prowess nerved his arm,
> It stands as fixed as Snowdon."—MASON.

Or, as Sir Walter Scott alludes to them,—

> "Some, chance-poised and balanced, lay
> So that a stripling arm might sway
> A mass no host could raise,
> In nature's rage at random thrown,
> Yet trembling like the Druid's Stone,
> On its precarious base."—LORD OF THE ISLES.

The council of Nantes, in the seventh century, ordered the bishops to have the rocking-stones destroyed. The coarse rose-coloured granite of this coast resembles the Egyptian.

We rowed back to the little inn at Ploumanach,

and had some eggs and a hot langouste or rock-lobster. This kind is more plentiful on the coast of Brittany than the common, but these rocky shores abound in both sorts. The village of Ploumanach is built nearly into the sea, in the midst of rocks overhanging the harbour. It is almost exclusively frequented by fishermen; in the front is a group of rocks or islands called Les Sept Iles; the Ile aux Moines, the most important among them, is strongly fortified, and is directly opposite Ploumanach. At the inn we found a German artist employed in making sketches in oil of this strange coast. It was late when we reached Lannion, a town prettily situated in the valley of Leguer; it contains no remarkable buildings except a few houses of the period of Henry IV. and Louis XIII. in the market-place. The mackerel and other fisheries are carried on from here, the grande and petite pêche, the " lieu " is taken in shoals and salted. The seaweed or wrack (*Fucus vesiculosus*), called goëmon, is extensively collected along the coasts of Brittany for fertilising the lands and also for fuel, which last is so scarce that even cow-dung is collected and dried against the walls for the same use. The gathering of goëmon takes place in March and September, and employs the whole population of the district. Souvestre says, that on the appointed day for gathering the crop, horses, oxen, cows, dogs, every animal, and every machine, is put into requisition. Women and children all are assembled in the bays, sometimes to the number of 10,000 persons; but, to allow the poor to have the full advantage, the custom is, on the first day, to admit only the necessitous of the parish. These borrow their neighbours' vehicles, and collect a good crop. It is called "the day of the poor." The goëmon grows on rocks at a distance from the shore, and the peasants not having sufficient boats to collect it tie the heaps together with cords on to branches of trees and form a raft, on which the whole family is launched; a barrel is attached at the end, and the unsteady craft often rolls over and its cargo is precipitated into the water. The fine sands of the sea shore are also carted and laid on the heavy lands to divide the soil. Ascending the valley of the Leguer, about eight miles from Lannion, on the opposite side of the river, we turned down a muddy lane, and getting out into a field saw in front of us the imposing castle of Tonquédec, perhaps the finest remains in Brittany of military architecture, dating from the fourteenth century. It crowns the summit of a hill, wooded down to the river's edge, with water-mills and a little village at the foot, the bright sparkling river running through the deep wild valley; nothing can exceed the picturesque effect of these ruins when seen from the opposite bank. Tonquédec has belonged from time immemorial to the Viscomtes de Coëtmen, who held the first rank among the nobles of Brittany, but one of them espousing the cause of the Constable Clisson against Duke John IV. saw his fortress demolished. It was restored under Henry IV., and again dismantled by order of Cardinal Richelieu, who hated castles and their nobility. The castle is an irregular four-sided figure. It had an outer enclosure, and was entered by a drawbridge, and furnished with every imaginable fortification. Three sides were surrounded by dwellings, among these a fine roofed salle d'armes remains. A flying bridge led to the keep, which was of four stories, but the entrance on the first story, so that in case of siege the garrison might retire to the keep, and hold out till want of provisions or ammunition compelled them to surrender. The towers and walls remain, the latter are ten feet thick.

On our way to Plouaret we drove up to the château of Kergrist, a square edifice with pepper-box towers at each angle, in good preservation, occupied by a lady of the name of Douglas. Our driver could not find the way to the "Chapelle des Sept Saints," built over a dolmen, which lay near the station at Plouaret, whence we proceeded by rail, and, entering the department of Finistère, shortly after reached Morlaix over its magnificent granite viaduct, the most important among the many which occur between Rennes and Brest. The railway runs parallel to the coast, and traverses, not far from their mouths, the streams which abound in this "pays accidenté." This gigantic work is one-sixth of a mile (292 yards) long, and consists of two tiers of arches, fourteen in the upper line and nine below.

Morlaix is picturesquely built on the sides of three ravines, so steep that the saying goes, "De la mansarde au jardin, comme on dit à Morlaix." It is situated on a tidal river, about eight miles from the sea, ascended by small vessels, which give the place a lively appearance. Few towns have so many beautiful timbered houses of the fifteenth and sixteenth centuries remaining. One of the most curious is that belonging to a miller, No. 19, in the Rue des Nobles, a street where the houses are built one story projecting over the other, so that the top stories of the opposite houses nearly touch each other and exclude the light. The fronts, gable-shaped, have their enormous beams richly carved, and supported by brackets and statues of St. Yves or other favourite saints; some are overlaid with lozenge-shaped slates, and finished at the point with a leaden "épi," or ornamental terminal. All have a kind of hall, panelled and sculptured to the roof, the staircases richly sculptured and supported by a pillar carved from top to bottom with statues of saints or grotesque figures superposed one over the other. Among the statuettes in the house, No. 19, are the figures of St. Roch and his dog; St. Christopher carrying the infant Jesus, St. Michael, and various others. On another staircase, in better preservation, but not so richly carved (at the Veuve Perron's, No. 14, Grande Rue), are female saints,—the Virgin, St. Catherine, and St. Barbara.

Morlaix gave a grand reception to the Queen-Duchess Anne, when on her pilgrimage through Brittany in 1505. The town presented her with a little ship of gold, bearing the arms of the city, and enriched with precious stones, and a tame ermine with a diamond collar round its neck. Anne received the ermine, and caressed the little animal, who returned her endearments, and, at length, suddenly concealed itself in her bosom, which unexpected proceeding startled the Queen, when the Seigneur du Rohan, who was by her side, exclaimed, "What do you fear, madam; is not the ermine your cognisance?" No less enthusiastic was the reception given by the citizens of Morlaix forty years later (1548) to Mary Stuart, then only five years old, on her landing in France. She was lodged in the convent of the Jacobins, and assisted at the Te Deum in the church of Notre Dame-du-

Mur. When passing through one of the gates on her way back, the drawbridge, overloaded with spectators, gave way, and several persons were thrown into the water. Mary's Scottish attendants cried out "Treason!" but the Seigneur de Rohan, who was on horseback by the side of the royal litter, indignantly exclaimed, "Jamais Breton ne fit trahison." The loyalty and good faith of the Bretons is proverbial. "En tout chemin, loyauté," is a Breton motto,[1] and it is one of the virtues attributed to them by a Breton writer, who assigns to them four virtues and three vices. Their virtues consist in a love of their country and their home, resignation to the will of the Almighty, loyalty to each other, and hospitality. Their vices are avarice, contempt for women, and drunkenness. Their love of country and home is carried to an extent, rivalling, if not exceeding, that of the Swiss. The Breton not only loves the village where he was born, but he loves the field of his fathers, the hearth and the clock of his home, even the bed on which he was born, and on which he hopes to close his eyes. The conscript and sailor are often known to die of grief when away from their native land. Brittany possesses for its children an inconceivable attraction, and there is no country in the

---

[1] E pess hænt lealdet!

world where man is more attached to his native soil.

> "O landes ! ô forêts ! pierres sombres et hautes,
> Bois qui couvrez nos champs, mers qui battez nos côtes,
> Villages où les morts errent avec les vents,
> Bretagne, d'où vient l'amour de tes enfants ?"—BRIZEUX.

The Bretons are brave soldiers and good sailors; their disposition is hasty and violent, and even ferocious in anger. When the people of Nantes rose up in rebellion against Duke Francis, his brother-in-law, the Comte du Foix, sent to pacify them, said to him on his return from his mission, " J'aimerais mieux être prince d'un million de sangliers que de tel peuple que sont vos Bretons "— Brittany has always been the theatre of great virtues and great crimes.

On Sunday we went to the Welsh Baptist Chapel, to hear Mr. Jenkins preach in the Breton language. He has been there thirty years zealously labouring among the peasants, to convert whom he was sent by the Welsh Baptist Missionary Society. From his thorough knowledge of the French and Breton languages, he is eminently fitted for the task. He travels about the surrounding country preaching, and establishing schools, and has revised the Breton[1] translation of the New Testament for the Society, and circulated, by means of colporteurs, from eight

---

[1] By Légonedec.

to nine thousand Bibles, besides above 100,000 tracts. The task of acquiring the Breton language is less difficult for a Welshman, for the similarity between them is so great that the two people are able to make themselves understood to each other. The labours of Mr. Jenkins have lately awakened the attention of the Breton Roman Catholic clergy, who have publicly denounced him from their altars, but without causing him to slacken in the good work he has undertaken. Persecuted by a tyrannical priesthood, who hold dominion over a peasantry bigoted in proportion to their ignorance, his position is one of difficulty and danger; but he goes on with undrooping energy, convinced that, though the progress is slow, the good seed has not been sown in vain, and will, in due time, bear fruit, though those who first sowed it may have passed away. There were about a dozen Bretons at the evening service; they seemed to be constantly going in and out, as if unable to keep up their attention to so long a service. There are also English Protestant chapels at Morlaix and Quimper, and French at Brest and Lorient.

We saw a christening in the cathedral, of a child about eighteen months old; the mother wore a wonderful conical cap of lace.

A few houses from our hotel a ball was going on, given every week for the workpeople of the town.

The clatter of their iron-pointed wooden shoes seemed quite to drown the music.

Next day we walked to the Fontaine des Anglais, so-called from the slaughter of a body of English at that place. Jealous of the prosperity of Morlaix, Henry VIII. sent a fleet up the river to attack the place, and the commander, being informed by a spy of the absence of the chief nobles at Guingamp, and of the townsmen at the fair of Pontivy, landed with a force which entered Morlaix, burnt it, and returned laden with booty to their boats. Six or seven hundred men, who were intoxicated, fell asleep in the wood, where they were attacked by the nobles, who had hastened from Guingamp to the assistance of the town, and were all massacred. The neighbouring fountain, said to have been tinged with the invaders' blood, received in memory of the event the name of "Fontaine des Anglais." It was on this occasion the town of Morlaix added to its arms, a lion (emblem of vigilance), encountering a two-headed leopard (for England), with the punning motto, "S'ils te mordent, mors-les" (Morlaix).

Emile Souvestre, author of 'Le Foyer Breton,' and 'Les Derniers Bretons,' the ablest portrayer of Breton manners, customs, and superstitions, was a native of Morlaix; he died in the Protestant Communion, 1854.

We were recommended to sail down the Morlaix River to its mouth, as the scenery is very picturesque, but we had not time to effect it. The great beauty of Brittany generally consists in its river scenery, the Rance, to Dinan; the rivers of Quimper and Quimperlé; the Aven, Elorn, and Blavet, are all highly picturesque and worth visiting. Our next drive was to St. Pol de Léon, partly along the bank of the river, passing under the church of Notre Dame-de-la-Salzette and the convent below of St. François. The tall steeples of St. Pol are seen at a great distance, and looking behind is the best view of the Mené-Bré, an insulated conical mountain, one of the Mené-Arré chain, situated near the station of Belle-Isle-Bégard. A chain of mountains runs through the Côtes-du-Nord, and, at the western end of the department, forks off into two branches which traverse the whole of Finistère, —the Mené-Arré, or northern chain, and the Montagnes Noires, or southern.

St. Pol looks like a town of the Middle Ages. "The holy city," as it is called by the Léonnais, one of the four bishoprics[1] into which Brittany was divided, comprising the modern districts of Morlaix and Brest. The Pays de Léon is remarkable for

---

[1] St. Pol de Léon, Cornouaille, Vannes et Tréguier.

the number of its religious monuments, its fine churches, its bone-houses, calvarys, way-side crosses, and shrines. Crosses are set up in every direction, and of every description, from the plain unpretending simple cross of wood or stone, to the huge crosses flaunting in green paint, with tears of gold—specimens of the taste of the maire or priest of the district. No Breton passes the sacred symbol without kneeling to salute it, and making the sign of the cross—evidence that the piety of those who first raised them has not degenerated in their posterity. The country is rich and varied. The Léonnais is tallest of all the Breton race; his dress is generally black or blue, with a coloured scarf round his waist, his hair is worn very long, and his broad-brimmed hat has a silver buckle. He is grave, of a calm confiding faith, which nothing can shake or alter, and of intense religious feeling. The church is the place of meeting, where all his business is transacted, all his aspirations centered. Throughout Brittany the priesthood are low and ignorant. Like the Irish, the Breton farmer's great ambition is to make his son a priest. In no part of France are they more uneducated than in Brittany.

St. Pol is still and melancholy, the grass grows in the streets, the city looks as if it had not awakened since its palmy days of the fourteenth century. Its churches, calvarys, cemeteries, all silent as death—

" A deep, still pool in the ocean of life."

Its lively neighbour, Morlaix, offers a strange contrast: its inhabitants may well say they are three hundred years in advance of St. Pol.

The pride of St. Pol de Léon is the church of Notre Dame-de-Creizker. Its steeple, nearly 400 feet high, was said by Vauban to be the boldest piece of architecture he ever beheld. It is built in the centre of the church, entirely of granite, cut in the shape of tiles and open work, to within eighty feet from the base. According to the legend, on the spot where the church now stands, there lived in the time of St. Génévroc, a young girl, whom the saint found, when passing her house on the fête of our Lady, employed at her needle. He reproached her gently with her impiety, yet she went on sewing, saying "she required food on Sundays as well as on work days." But the girl has hardly finished speaking, when all her body became cold and motionless as a stone. She was completely paralysed. Asking pardon of St. Génévroc, he made the sign of the cross upon each of her limbs, and the power of motion returned. Grateful for her recovery, she gave to the saint, her house, which was situated in the middle of the town (as its name implies), as a site for his church. It is said to have been built by an English architect, invited to Brittany by Mary Plantagenet, daughter of Edward III., and first wife of Duke John IV.[1]

The axis of the nave is inclined to the left, a mystic allusion to the position of the head of the expiring Saviour on the cross. *Et inclinato capite, emise spiritum,* " And He bowed his head, and gave up the ghost." The north porch of the Creizker is beautifully sculptured with leaves of the mallow, the vine, and mulberry. It was all under repair when we saw it.

The cathedral has two fine towers with spires, and a magnificent rose window of the fifteenth century in the south transept, with, above, the "fenêtre d'excommunication." The fine porch, lightly and delicately sculptured, is surmountd by a balustrade, whence the episcopal benediction was given. Over the high altar is a large wooden crosier, gilt, from which to suspend the ciborium, similar to that we saw in the cathedral of Dol. A black marble slab, at the foot of the steps of the high altar, marks the grave of St. Pol de Léon, who died 570. St. Pol, the patron bishop and founder of the cathedral, was

---

[1] His second wife was also English, Jane Holland, half-sister of Richard II.; his third, Joan, daughter of Charles the Bad, King of Navarre, who afterwards married Henry IV. of England.

The Creisker.

one of the clergy of Great Britain who emigrated to Brittany in the sixth century; he landed in the island of Ouëssant, and passed on to the country of Léon, where he founded a monastery. The island of Batz was, at that time, infested by an enormous dragon, sixty feet long; the saint, accompanied by a warrior, entered the cavern of the monster, tied his stole round its neck, and gave him to his companion to lead, St. Pol following, beating him with his stick, till they arrived at the extremity of the island, when he took off the stole, and commanded the dragon to throw itself in the sea, an order the animal immediately obeyed. St. Pol is always represented with the dragon by his side, the stole round its neck. We were shown a little bell, said to have belonged to the saint. It appears he had repeatedly asked the king to give him this bell for his new church, but had always been refused. When one day some fishermen brought him a large fish taken off the island of Batz, and in its mouth was the coveted bell. It is certainly very ancient in form, a kind of square pyramid about four inches wide and nine high, of beaten red copper mixed, we were told, with a considerable quantity of silver. It is now rung over the heads of the faithful on pardons, as a specific against headache and earache—a singular remedy! The cathedral has a fine marble tomb of Bishop Visdelou, preacher to Queen Anne of

Austria; he is represented in a half reclining posture, in his pontifical garments. In every part of the cathedral are the little boxes of skulls.

Adjacent is the Ursuline convent, where is preserved a small figure of the Virgin in jet; brought from a church in the Iles Sainte Marguerite, taken from the Spaniards in the seventeenth century. It is supposed to possess miraculous powers, and is sent round to the sick as a specific.

We breakfasted at the little inn (Hôtel de France), commanding a pretty view of the coast from its windows and garden. The Léon country was governed by Viscounts, who boasted, among several manorial rights, the " droit de motte," which empowered them, if a vassal (they were "serfs de motte") attempted to live out of his demesne, or to enter the service of another lord, to bring him back to his "motte," a cord round his neck, and inflict upon him corporal punishment. By virtue of the same right, if the demesne of a lord was so placed that it had no natural height from which to survey its extent, his vassals were made to bring sufficient cart-loads of earth to raise a mound or "motte" of the requisite elevation. The other privilege was the droit de "bris," equivalent to our flotsum and jetsum, so lucrative that a Léon Viscount is recorded to have said, when a noble was exhibiting his casket of gems, that he possessed a jewel more precious than all they were admiring—alluding to a rock famous for its shipwrecks. Duke John the Red, taking advantage of the misdeeds of one of these lords of Léon, seized his rich possessions and united them (1276) to the crown. The viscounty of Léon fell by alliance, in the fourteenth century, to the house of Rohan, in whose favour is was raised in the sixteenth to a principality.

We continued our drive to Roscoff, three miles distant, a little sea-port town, formerly one of the three great dens of corsairs and smugglers, all under the protection of St. Barbe,—the other two being Camaret and Le Conquet. Roscoff was the emporium of considerable contraband trade with England. Tea, wine, and brandy were brought over in small casks, which the smugglers tied together and threw into the sea, when near the coast, and landed at night. The whole country round is now one extent of kitchen-garden, the light sandy soil, dressed with the goëmon, produces an incredible quantity of vegetables, onions, cabbages, parsnips, asparagus, artichokes, cauliflowers, &c. Of onions, 2,000,000 lbs. are said to be sent every year to England alone. The people here wear black caps, those of the men are stocking-knit. The gardeners of Roscoff will carry their produce above a hundred miles for sale. The chief vegetable consumed by the Bretons themselves is the cabbage, of which the quantity raised is enormous. The kind grown is mostly the Jersey or cow-cabbage, which grows with stalks from five to six feet high, and has large leaves at every joint. They use them for their cattle, as well as for their own eating. Avenues of cabbages, stacked five or six feet high, are to be seen in most Breton markets. Bread or porridge of buckwheat (blé noir) with cabbage-soup is the customary diet of the country. The recipe is simple, consisting of a cabbage-leaf, over which a little hot water is thrown, and a "soupçon" of butter added to give it a flavour. These ingredients compose the national soup which always appears at the tâble d'hôte, with the inevitable "ragoût," *i. e.* harricoed mutton.

The little town of Roscoff has some historic importance. It was here that John de Montfort sailed to England to do homage to King Edward III. for the duchy of Brittany, and returned by the same port. Here also the child-princess Mary Stuart landed in 1548 to marry the young Dauphin, afterwards Francis II. In commemoration of the event, she afterwards caused the little chapel of St. Ninian to be built close on the water's edge. It is not more than fifty feet long, and has an eastern flamboyant window, with others in the side walls. The arches are fast going to decay, the stone altar is also sculptured. When we saw it, the interior was filled with bundles of broom-branches and poultry.

It is strange this little chapel, built by the Queen of two Kingdoms, should be suffered to fall to ruin for the lack of a trifling outlay.

Here, two hundred years later, Prince Charles Stuart landed after Culloden, in the French frigate the 'Heureux,' sent by the French Government to facilitate his escape, having eluded, through the chances of a fog, the pursuit of the English cruisers; and here he knelt, in the chapel of his ancestress, to return thanks for his deliverance.

The church of Roscoff has a curious pierced steeple, like many of those in Finistère, and some alabaster bas-reliefs of the fourteenth century, with numerous boxes of skulls. A ship rudely sculptured by the porch, and another by the east window, show that the fishermen and ship-owners contributed to the building of the church. By the shore is a rock of grotesque form, and opposite, about three miles from Roscoff, is the pretty island of Batz, which derives its name—Breton "batz," a stick—from the rod used by St. Pol de Léon to work his miracle.

People were busily employed in boats collecting the goëmon, which they pile in heaps along the shore. The great curiosity of Roscoff is its enormous fig-tree, in the garden of the Capucine convent, said to be two centuries old. It is supported by stone pillars, and is, we were informed, above 300 feet in circumference.

We returned that evening to Morlaix: the viaduct by moonlight had a most picturesque appearance. Next morning we proceeded by rail to the station of St. Thégonnec, where nothing in the shape of a vehicle was to be had to convey us to the town— nearly a mile and a half distant—but the ricketty two-wheeled mail cart. At the little cabaret, which bears the important name of Hôtel de la Grande Maison, we procured breakfast. The church has been restored. It is rich in carvings, spoiled by gilding, the altars and canopied pulpit especially. Opposite to the last are two coloured "retables." The high altar, with two side altars and two smaller ones behind, are gorgeously carved, coloured and gilt, and extend to the roof. The painted-glass windows are the gifts of various persons. At the entrance of the churchyard is a Renaissance porch, or triumphal arch, dated 1581, with a sculpture representing St. Thégonnec, a bullock and car by his side. Adjoining, is the ossuary, or reliquary, bearing the date 1676, also in the same elaborate style, destitute of bones, but having below a crypt containing a group of life-sized figures representing the Entombment, with this inscription:—

"Tu le vois mort, pécheur, ce Dieu qui t'a fait naître:
Sa mort est ton ouvrage, et devient ton appui.
A ce trait de bonté, tu dois au moins vivre pour lui."

In the churchyard is also a calvary; the name given

to those monumental sculptures peculiar to Brittany, consisting of the crucifix, surrounded by the chief witnesses of the crucifixion, together with minor groups representing passages in the life of our Saviour. This calvary, executed in Kersanton stone, is dated 1610; the numerous figures are all in the grotesque costume of the period, with ruffs, toquets, trained gowns, and scalloped jackets.

We took a carriage for Guimiliau, passing on our road to the left, a grotto. The church of Guimiliau partly dates from the Renaissance; it has a finely sculptured porch, and contains within carvings of great beauty; the pulpit, supported on a column, is dated 1677; the organ-loft is enriched with splendid bas-reliefs in oak panels,—one represents a triumphal march, after Le Brun, the others, King David and St. Cecilia. But the grand monumental carving is the magnificent baptistery or baptismal font, surmounted by a baldachin or canopy, supported by eight twisted columns interlaced with vines, grapes and flowers, with graceful little birds pecking the fruit. On the top of the canopy is a dolphin, and above, two figures of Fame, trumpet-mouthed, surmounted by a royal crown and the letters S. V. This baptistery and the organ-loft are both in the style of Louis XIV., and are said to have cost 30,000 francs. In the churchyard are a triumphal arch and a reliquary, both inferior to those of St. Thégonnec, but the calvary of Guimiliau is one of the most extensive in Brittany. It is of the sixteenth century. It consists of a solid platform, ascended by a stair-

23.   Calvary, Guimiliau.

case, and raised upon arches; upon it, sculptured in Kersanton stone, are the three crosses, the centre one beautifully carved with St. John and the Virgin

Mary by the side. The four Evangelists are placed at each corner, and all the passages in the life of Christ are represented by groups of little figures in the costume of the sixteenth century. This singular monument bears two different dates, those of 1581 and 1588.

Guimiliau is close to the railway, but there is no station there. We returned to St. Thégonnec. The peasants along the road were threshing their buckwheat on the open ground; women as well as men were at work. They threshed in a circle, keeping good time with their strokes, and laughing merrily while they flourished their flails,—they appeared a most joyous party,—

> "Ho! batteux, battons la gerbe,
> Compagnons, joyeusement."

Buckwheat, their "blé noir," is the Breton's chief food, and is cultivated to a large extent. With its coral-red stalks and snowy flowers it has a very pretty appearance growing, and is the first care of the Breton farmer—

> "Ah! que la sombre nue aux funestes lueurs,
>   Planant sur la campagne,
> Epargne les blés-noirs, les blés aux blanches fleurs,
>   Ce pain de la Bretagne."—STÉPHANE HALGAN.

This plant, a native of Asia Minor, was evidently, from its French name, "sarrazin," introduced into Europe by the Saracens or Moors. We proceeded by rail to Brest, passing under the foot of the abrupt rock upon which stand the picturesque ruins of the ancient castle of La Roche Maurice and the church of La Roche. The rail runs along the banks of the Elorn through a narrow wooded valley; the windings of the river are very picturesque, and formerly a steamer ran from Landerneau to Brest, affording the opportunity of seeing them.

Brest, the first harbour in France, is Breton only in name and locality; it is built in an amphitheatre on the slopes of two hills divided by the river Penfeld, which forms the port. On the right is the suburb Recouvrance, on the left Brest proper. This irregular site often causes the second floor of the houses in one street to be on a line with the ground floor of another. Brest is clean and well built, and consists of three long parallel streets. The principal one, called the Rue de Siam, in commemoration of the Siamese Ambassadors sent to Louis XIV., who landed here, runs the whole length of the town, ending at the fine iron bridge called the Pont Impériale, the largest swing-bridge ever constructed. You descend by a flight of steps from the Rue de Siam to the lower streets. Running along the bay, of considerable extent, and well planted with trees, is the magnificent promenade called the Cours d'Ajot, from the name of the officer of the Engineers by whom it was laid out and planted a century back. Well sheltered by its trees and refreshed by the sea breezes, it commands a fine view over the new "port de commerce," and the whole extent of the harbour of Brest, which is capable of containing 500 ships of the line, and is, with the exception of those of Rio Janeiro and Constantinople, the largest and most beautiful in the world.

Brest harbour has only one entrance, which is to the west, through a narrow channel called Le Goulet, less than a mile in width, and cut into two by the Mingant rock. In the year 1796 the 'Republican' was lost here. Sailing out of the harbour, with a contrary wind and snow, the pilot thought he had passed the Mingant rock, when the ship struck, and went down with 800 men on board. Brest Castle in the Middle Ages was a place of such strength and importance that John IV., who had four times besieged it fruitlessly, when it was under the English dominion, was wont to say "Ce n'est duc de Bretagne, qui n'est pas sire de Brest." It had been held by Sir Robert Knolles against the army of the King of France under Du Guesclin, who was obliged to raise the siege. The donjon was built by King Richard II. during the War of Succession. The making Brest an important naval station was the thought of Richelieu, and the work of Louis XIV., who built the arsenal.

Next day we made an excursion to see the church of Notre Dame-du-Folgoët or the Fool of the Wood, celebrated in legendary lore: the tale is so old and often told, we have some scruples in repeating it.

Towards the middle of the fourteenth century, there lived in the woods of Lesneven, a poor idiot boy, called Salaun (Solomon), better known under the name of the Fool of the Wood (Folgoët). He was miserably clad, had no bed but the ground; no pillow, but a stone; no roof, but the tree which gave him shelter. He went every day to Lesneven to seek his daily bread, but he never begged; he uttered the simple words "Ave Maria! Solomon could eat bread," and returned with whatever pittance was given him to his tree near the fountain, into which he dipped his crusts, and plunged even in the depth of winter, for his bath, always repeating the words, "Hail, Maria!" One day a party of marauding soldiers accosted him. In answer to their questions, he replied, "I am neither for Blois nor Montfort, I am the servant of the Lady Mary." This simple life he led for nearly forty years, when at last he fell ill and died, repeating his favourite words "Ave Maria." He was found dead near the fountain, and was buried by his neighbours. After a time, when the memory of the poor idiot boy had nearly passed away, there suddenly sprung up from his grave a white lily with the words " Ave Maria" inscribed in letters of gold upon its petals. The news of the miracle spread throughout all Brittany, Duke John sent commissioners; the grave was opened, and it was found the lily proceeded from the mouth of Salaun,—" ceste royale fleur sortait par sa bouche du creux de son estomach"—a testimony of the innocence and piety "du plus beau mignon de la reine des Cieux." Duke John vowed to erect a church to our Lady over the fountain of the poor mendicant, whose faith had been thus recognised;[1] and, faithful to his promise, the first stone was laid by him in 1366, as a thank-offering for his success the previous year at the battle of Auray, which had fixed the crown upon his head. His wife, Joan of Navarre, not only made a pilgrimage to the Folgoët in 1396, but also contributed to the building of the church. It was completed by John V., about 1419. The Queen-Duchess Anne of Brittany went there in pilgrimage

---

[1] "Venu au monde à l'époque où naissait Bertrand Du Guesclin, enlevé au ciel à l'époque du combat des Trente, Salaun fit moins de bruit sur la terre que le célèbre Connétable ou que les braves compagnons de Beaumanoir. Son corps ne fut pas transporté en pompe royale à S. Denis, pour y reposer au milieu des souverains; aucun obélisque ne rappelle sa mémoire : mais sur son humble tombe on a construit un monument qui fire vivre son nom dans la suite des siècles. C'est que Salaun, loin de chercher l'agitation des combats, ne demande que le calme de la prière. Il choisit la meilleure part, et il ne fut pas otée."—POL DE COURCY.

after the recovery from illness of Louis XIII. Anne of Austria founded six masses at the Folgoët, in gratitude for the birth of Louis XIV., and several popes granted indulgences to those who made pilgrimages to this shrine. This church is one of the finest in Brittany. Its colour is sombre; it is the oldest monument in Brittany in which the Kersanton stone is employed. This stone is a volcanic rock called hornblende, of very fine grain, with minute specks of mica. There is a large quarry near St. Pol de Léon; but it is found principally on the west of the harbour of Brest, near a village from which it takes its name. Kersanton stone is of a dark-green colour, approaching to bronze, gives out a metallic sound when struck, and is easily worked in the quarry, in blocks of from twenty to forty feet cube, but hardens on exposure to the air. Time has no destructive effect on it; the most delicate, lightest, and most ornamental sculptures executed in it remain uninjured, while the hardest granites, erected at the same time, are friable and decomposed. The Kersanton stone cuts glass like a diamond.

The architecture of the Folgoët is distinguished for the elegance and richness of its ornamentation: the softness of the Kersanton stone, when fresh taken from the quarry fits it specially for the deeply cut, lace-like works of the artists of the flamboyant school, and the church is remarkable for the skill with which the productions of the vegetable kingdom are represented both within and without. It has no transepts, but to the south is a projection formed by the treasure chamber. The modern pulpit has a series of medallion bas-reliefs representing the legend of Solomon.

The jubé, or roodloft, is a perfect lacework of stone. Above three arches, decorated with vine-leaves, is an open-worked gallery of pierced quatrefoils surpassing in exuberance of ornament any other known.

To the east are five altars, all of Kersanton stone, most delicately sculptured—the under-cutting of the foliage most wonderful. They are in the shape of tombs or sarcophagi, the form generally adopted for altars in the sixteenth century. Round the "autel des anges," richest of them all, is a row of eighteen niches, filled in with the figures of angels, holding alternately phylacteries and escutcheons; round the top is a cornice of thistle-leaves—on the cut stalk of one hangs a dew-drop perfect to nature.

The high altar is decorated with vine-leaves, birds pecking the grapes, and the ermine, with its motto "À ma vie," introduced. The altar of the rosary has also a cornice of vine-leaves modelled evidently after the high altar.

The fine flamboyant rose window at the east of

the church resembles that of St. Pol de Léon, and below it is the fountain of Salaun. The spring is concealed under the high altar, and flows into a basin without, preserved by a kind of Gothic porch

24.   The Fool's Well, Folgoët.

sculptured with thistle-leaves and crockets, and within it, on a bracket, is a delicately chiseled image of the Virgin. Some children round the fountain offered us pins, the use of which we did not understand. We afterwards learned that it is the custom in Brittany for girls to take a pin from their bodice, and throw it into a sacred well, to ascertain, by its manner of sinking, when they would be married. If the pin falls head foremost, then there is no present hope of matrimony, but if the point goes first, it is a sure sign of being married that year.

On the new year, in some parts of Brittany, pieces of bread-and-butter are thrown into the fountains, and from the way in which they swim the future is foretold. If the buttered side turns under, it forebodes death; if two pieces adhere together, it is a sign of sickness; and if the piece floats, it is an assurance of long life and happiness.

The veneration for springs and healing wells is of very ancient date, and was prohibited by early councils of the Church; but the worship of that element from which suffering humanity seeks for relief in all its ailments has passed through succeeding creeds, and that which was held sacred a thousand years back is still the object of reverence and affection.

Nor is the sculpture outside the church less remarkable than the interior. The west door, now fallen to decay, has an arch with double entrance separated by a column containing a bénitier. A wreath of curled leaves runs round the arch, and on a bracket of thistle-leaves formerly stood a statue of John V.

The north side has little ornament. The great richness is in the south, where is the fine porch of Bishop Alain de la Rue, who consecrated the building, and more splendid still, is, at the angle formed by the projecting sacristy facing the west, the Porch of the Apostles. The twelve Apostles are ranged on each side, under rich canopies; the whole porch one mass of floral decoration, vine-leaves and mallows, interspersed with dragons, birds, and insects. On the right of the porch is a crouching figure with a label inscribed: "Bn soiez venz,"—"Bien soiez venuz" or "Soyez les bien venus"—an invitation to the faithful to enter into the church. On the lintel of the two doors are ermines passant, and the motto of the Dukes of Brittany, "À ma vie," and towards the south are the remains of a whole cornice of ermines, running through the rings of a long scroll inscribed with "À ma vie." This motto was first taken by Duke John IV. (who instituted the order of the Ermine) to imply that he had conquered Brittany, and would maintain it, even at the cost of his life, "à ma vie."[1]

---

[1] Duke Francis I. subsequently united the order of the Ermine with that of the "Epi;" and the collar was then composed of ears of corn, with an ermine pendant, and the motto of Duke John.

The collar consisted of a double chain, in each of which were four ermines, and two more hung suspended from two chains, surmounted by coronets. The motto "À ma vie" was placed round each of these ten ermines. The Père Lobineau quotes a history of Duke John, in which the order is thus spoken of:—

> "Lors fit mander tous les Prélats,
> Abbés et Clercs de tous Estats,
> Barons, Chevaliers, Escuyers,
> Qui tous portoient nouveaux Colliers
> De moult bel port et belle guise ;
> Et étoit nouvelle Dévise
> De deux Rolets brunis et beaux,
> Couplés ensemble de deux fermeaux ;
> Et au dessus étoit l'Ermine
> En figure et en couleur fine,
> En deux Cedules avoit escript
> À ma vie, comme j'ai dit ;
> L'un mot est blanc, l'autre noir,
> Il est certain, tien, pour le voir."

In the churchyard is a cross erected by Cardinal de Coëtivy (died 1474), who is represented kneeling at the foot; it is said to be the work of Michel Colomb, sculptor of the celebrated monument raised by Queen Anne of Brittany to her parents, now in the Cathedral at Nantes. Next day, we went to Le Conquet, returning by St. Mathieu. We crossed the swing-bridge to the suburb Recouvrance, so called from the chapel of our Lady, to whom shipwrecked mariners addressed their petitions to recover (recouvrir) their property. On our left we saw the islet rock of Bertheaume, about 200 feet high, distant from the coast 150. Until lately, the communication with the mainland was by means of a kind of cradle drawn on two cables, about nine mètres in circumference.

Le Conquet[1] is a little seaport built on the slope of a steep hill. Formerly it was of some importance, and a great resort of pirates. Sir Walter Manny took the town for the Countess of Montfort, during the war of the two Jeannes, and it was attacked by the fleets of Henry VIII. and his daughter Mary. Opposite is a beautiful beach, called the Blancs Sablons, accessible at low water by walking across the harbour. Here is the point of communication with the island of Ouëssant, about seventeen miles distant, by means of a steamer, weather permitting, as the Chenal du Four, which separates this group of islands from the continent, is covered with rocks and is very dangerous in rough weather. Its men are all seamen or fishermen, the women perform the agricultural labour. They bring in their produce to Brest at the monthly fairs, and are not so cut off from the world as Gresset describes them:—

---

[1] The word *cong*, in ancient Breton, means a basin surrounded by quays, to receive and protect vessels from wind and sea—as Conquet, Concarneau, or Cong-kernay.

> "Sous un ciel toujours rigoureux
> Au sein des flots impétueux,
> Non loin de l'Armorique plage
> Habitacle marécageux,
> Moitié peuplé, moitié sauvage,
> Dont les habitants malheureux
> Separés du reste du monde,
> Semblent ne connoître l'onde
> Et n'être connus que des cieux."
>
> <div align="right">Gresset.—<i>Carême impromptu.</i></div>

We now reached the Abbey of St. Mathieu, situated on the extreme point of Brittany and of France, on the top of a promontory, well called Finistère. Here in the sixth century was built a monastery in honour of St. Matthew the Evangelist, whose head had been stolen in Egypt by some Breton navigators, and been brought to land at this point, which long bore the name of " St. Mathieu de fin de terre " (Finistère). In the twelfth century the monastery was converted into a Benedictine abbey, which is a beautiful example of the Early English style. The formidable rocks at its feet are called Les Moines. The monks of St. Mathieu kept a beacon for the safety of mariners on these dangerous shores. The modern lighthouse quite masks the sight of the abbey, and is a great disfigurement to the view, which, in other respects, is most grand; the imposing granite ruins of the abbey church on the very edge of these weather-beaten cliffs, worn and torn by the ocean with its unwearied waves; on the right, the reefs of the Passage du Four, which appear to unite the islands of Ouëssant and its satellites to St. Mathieu; on the left the elongated point of the Bec du Raz, which no one, according to the Bretons, ever passed without grief and suffering. In sight of Saint Mathieu, the English in 1504, with eighty ships, attacked Hervé de Porzmoguer, a Breton captain, with only twenty. His own ship the 'Cordelière,' which had been built and fitted out by Anne of Bretagne, at her own expense, took fire; it held 1200 troops besides the ship's company. Porzmoguer grappled the 'Cordelière' to the ship of the English admiral, the 'Great Harry;' and both vessels, driven by the north-west wind to the entrance of the Goulet, were burned together, and above 2000 men perished in the two ships. Porzmoguer mounted the mast followed by the raging flames, and cast himself from the main-top, in full armour, into the sea.

In 1597, the fleet sent by Philip II. to take possession of Brittany for Spain was dispersed in a storm off Point St. Mathieu, and, out of a hundred and twenty ships, scarcely one remained.

On our way home, we passed a little town called La Trinité, from three springs all issuing from the same fountain, at which washerwomen with their wooden bats were hard at work, beating the clothes to rags on the stones.

25. Abbey of St. Mathieu.

Next day was the monthly fair at Brest, which brought in many of the country people in their picturesque costumes. Most conspicuous among them were the peasants of Ouëssant, last type of the

26.   Peasant Girl of Ouëssant.

Celtic women, in their singularly Italian-looking head-dress, their hair streaming over their shoulders; and the Plougastel men, in red caps, with coats and trowsers of white flannel.

Most of the market-women were furnished with

enormous umbrellas, red, blue, and green. In this rainy province, they are indispensable, and the acquisition of an umbrella is a great object of ambition to the Breton peasant.

We left Brest by the steamer for Pont Launay and Châteaulin, a four hours' sail in the harbour of Brest. On the right we passed the Point des Espagnols, where Frobisher, sent by Queen Elizabeth to the assistance of Henry IV., received his death wound. Leaving on our left Plougastel, where we were unable to visit the celebrated calvary, we passed near the " Anse du Fret," whence Joan of Navarre, then widow of Duke John IV., sailed to England to marry Henry of Lancaster, 1403. Henry, when Earl of Derby, had visited Nantes to ask the assistance of his uncle in returning to England, and Joan had favoured his expedition, but Duke John died the same year (1399). When Queen Dowager of England, she saw the children of her two husbands arrayed against each other, and her son Arthur, who had been invested by King Henry IV. with the Earldom of Richmond, made prisoner at Agincourt by his half-brother King Henry V., who confined him in the Tower, and afterwards in Fotheringay Castle. Joan received hard treatment from her stepson. Accused of being a sorceress—a reputation she inherited from her father, Charles the Bad of Navarre—Henry caused her to be confined in

Leeds and Pevensey castles, and deprived her of her property. It was only on his approaching death that he restored her to liberty. She retired to Havering Bower in Essex, where her grandson, the unfortunate Gilles de Bretagne, was reared and educated with Henry VI. She died in 1437, and the memory of "Joan the witch queen" was long held in awe by the people of Havering Bower.

On the left is the hamlet of Kersanton, which gives its name to the stone so called. At the entrance of the Aulne,[1] to the right, we passed the ruins of the abbey of Landévenec, the most ancient monastic establishment in Brittany. At Pont Launay an omnibus took us to the railway station at Châteaulin, celebrated for its slate quarries, a drive of three quarters of an hour. From here we proceeded by rail to Quimper, capital of Cornouaille. The district of Cornouaille—Cornu-Galliæ, expressing its position at the horn or extremity of France—is most varied in character. The part on the north is enclosed between the two chains of mountains, which, running nearly parallel with each other, traverse the department of Finistère, the Mené-Arré, and the Montagnes Noires. A single chain passes through the Côtes-

---

[1] A fine viaduct is in course of construction across the valley of the Aulne, composed of twelve arches, remarkable for their immense span (72 feet), and at an elevation of 170 feet above the water.

du-Nord, and forks off, at the edge of the department, near Callac, whence the northern range, the Mené-Arré, runs westwards to Faou harbour; while the Montagnes Noires incline to the south-west, and

27.   Peasant Girl, Châteaulin.

reach the sea near Crozon. The country between these chains is dreary and bare—barren plains and black mountains; to the south it is cultivated and productive. The stormy rock-bound coast is wild and desolate. One-third of the department consists of landes, marshes, and sandy shores (*grèves*). The people are the Irish of Brittany. Their wants are restricted to a tub of salted pork and a provision of cider, with rye, or black corn, to make their "galette." They are simple in their manners, kind to the poor, and enduring of suffering. Respect for the misfortunes of others, and patience under their own, is one of the Breton characteristics.

In the days of Conan Meriadec there lived a holy man, called Corentin, who retired to a solitude for prayer and meditation, near a fountain in a forest. Every morning a little fish came to him from the fountain; he cut a piece off it for his daily pittance and threw it again into the water, and in an instant the fish became whole. The miracle was repeated every morning. One day King Gradlon, who held his court at "Kemper," was in the forest near the hermitage of St. Corentin, with some of his suite, and asked him if he could give him something to eat. The saint immediately ran to his fountain and called his little fish, cut off a piece, which he gave to the maître d'hôtel to prepare for the king and his attendants. The chef laughed when he took the slice; but, to the surprise of everybody, the fish multiplied so as to completely satisfy the hunger of the king and his party. Gradlon threw himself on his knees at the feet of St. Corentin, and gave him the forest, with a "maison de plaisance," which St. Corentin converted into a monastery. The king afterwards erected Quimper into a bishopric, to which he nominated St. Corentin :—

> "Voici dans le fond la ville de Kemper,
> Asise au confluent de l'Oded et du Ster.
> Comme sa cathédrale, aux deux tours dentelées,
> S'élève noblement du milieu des vallées,
> O perle de l'Oded, fille du roi Grallon,
> Qui de saint Corentin portes aussi le nom,
> Rejouis-toi, Kemper, dans tes vielles murailles !
> Vois avec quelle ardeur, ô reine de Cornouailles,
> Tes fils de tous les points de l'antique évêché,
> Pêcheurs et montagnards, viennent à ton marché !
> Cornouillais ! en passant près de sa basilique,
> Du bon saint Corentin adorez la relique.
> Que tous ceux d'Elliant et des mêmes chemins
> Boivent à sa fontaine et s'y lavent les mains ;
> Non pas les Léonards, eux de qui les ancêtres,
> Voici quelque mille ans, hommes jaloux et traîtres,
> Volèrent le poisson dont notre Corentin
> Coupait pour se nourrir un peu chaque matin,
> Et qui chaque matin, ô pieuse merveille !
> Nageait dans sa fontaine aussi frais que la veille :
> Eh bien ! les Léonards volèrent ce poisson,
> Mais Kemper n'oublie jamais leur trahison ;
> Sans jouir de leur crime, ils en portent la peine,
> Et toujours le poisson nage dans la fontaine."
>
> *Les Bretons*—Brizeux.

Quimper, or Quimper-Corentin, is prettily situated at the junction of the rivers Odet and Stheire; its Breton name, Kemper, signifying confluence. It was long called Kemper-Odet. On the opposite side of the river the hills, consisting of a mass of rocks, covered with trees, rise to some height, and are ascended by well-kept walks. The river runs straight through the town, like a canal, edged by stone quays and crossed by iron bridges, with avenues of trees on each side. Trout can be seen in the sparkling stream; and we watched a boy with a hook at the end of a reel of black silk, hanging over the bridge, with a piece of kneaded bread for bait. With this simple tackle he contrived to hook a trout of tolerable size, and let it run out the length of his silk line till he had tired it out and landed it. The scenery of the river below Quimper, flowing through a bed of granite blocks, is, we were told, lovely, but we had no time to visit it further down. The view from the top of the wood-covered heights on the opposite side is very extensive, looking down upon the town, with its cathedral towers rising above, the promenade, and the course of the river. At the end of the town there is a manufactory of coarse pottery; but formerly it produced ware of a finer quality.

The beautiful cathedral is the largest of the four episcopal churches of Lower Brittany (Vannes, St. Pol, Quimper, and Tréguier), and was principally built in the fifteenth century. On the platform over the finely sculptured porch, rich in foliage like the Folgoët, placed between the two towers, is the equestrian statue of King Gradlon, to whom is attributed the introduction of the vine into Brittany. The statue was decapitated in 1793, but restored ten years back. On St. Cecilia's day companies of musicians used to mount on the platform. While they sang a hymn in praise of King Gradlon, one of the choristers, provided with a flagon of wine, a napkin, and golden hanap, mounted on the crupper of King Gradlon's horse, poured out a cup of wine, which he offered ceremoniously to the lips of the statue and then drank himself, carefully wiped with his napkin the moustachios of the king, placed a branch of laurel in his hand, and then threw down the hanap in the midst of the crowd below, in honour of the first planter of the grape in Brittany. To whoever caught the cup before it fell, and presented it uninjured to the Chapter, was adjudged a prize of two hundred crowns.

The two spires of the cathedral are modern, and were built by an annual subscription of a sou for five years, called the " sou du St. Corentin:" more than 600*l.* was thus raised. They have only been lately finished.

The men about Quimper all wear the national costume—enormous bragou-bras, or breeches of a kind of white sail-cloth, a broad-brimmed felt hat, long hair, falling over the shoulders, wooden shoes, and a broad belt with metal buckle. Their woollen jacket and waistcoat are edged with gay colours, and have sometimes the itinerant tailor's name and the date of the making of the garment, embroidered in wool upon the breast. On gala days brown or blue cloth bragous are worn, tied with coloured ribbons at the knees, black leather gaiters with buttons, and

28.   Beggar. Quimper.

the sabots are replaced by leather shoes and costly silver buckles. The national costume is more preserved in Cornouaille than in the other parts of Brittany. The pen bas or cudgel, with a large knob, like the Irish shillelah, is always ready at hand:—

> "Comme une conque immense ouverte au bord des eaux,
> En Cornouaille est un port, il y vient cent bateaux.
> Un sable jaune et fin couvre ses côtes plates,
> Mais un infect amas de rogues, de morgates,
> D'ossements de poissons sur le rivage épars,
> La saumure qui filtre entre ses deux remparts,
> Soulèvent tous les sens quand cette odeur saline
> Arrive au voyageur qui tourne la colline,
> Laissant derrière lui les taillis de Melven,
> La belle lande d'or qui parfume Aven,
> Et ces mouvants aspects de plaines, de montagnes
> Que déroulent sans fin nos sauvages campagnes.
> Plus de batteurs de seigle ici, plus de faucheurs,
> Mais des canots chargés de mousses, de pêcheurs,
> Partant et revenant avec chaque marée,
> Et sur les quais du pont versant à leur rentrée,
> Des sardines en tas, des congres, des merlus,
> Des homards cuirassés, de gros crabes velus;
> Et, du fond des paniers, mille genres énormes,
> De toutes les couleurs et de toutes les formes,
> Avec leur œil vitreux et leur museau béant,
> Tous enfants monstrueux du grand monstre Océan.
> Aussitôt le pressier les sèche, les empile,
> Et quand leur grasse chair a degorgé son huile,
> De Nantes à Morlaix cherchant les acheteurs,
> On voit bondir sur mer les hardis caboteurs."
>
> *Les Bretons*—BRIZEUX.

Thus the Breton poet describes Concarneau, a little fortified town, which has been called the St. Malo of Cornouaille, and is celebrated for its sardine fishery. The road lay through a wooded country, with steep hills and valleys, intersected by streams:

on the right a view of the Bay of La Forêt, where extensive oyster-culture is going on. After a tedious journey with miserable horses, we reached Concarneau at nine, a distance of little more than thirteen

29.   Concarneau, with Sardine Boats.

miles, having set off a few minutes after four. Concarneau proper is on a rocky island, surrounded by fortifications, with eight or nine towers and thick walls, and communicating with the mainland by means of a drawbridge. This is called the "Ville Close." It consists of only one street. When Duke John IV. embarked from here for England, he left

Sir Robert Knollys governor of the duchy. The constable Du Guesclin, after the surrender of Hennebont and Quimperlé, took Concarneau by storm and slew all the English garrison, except the captain, who received quarter.

Opposite the island is the faubourg Sainte Croix, which is more populous than the Ville Close, and where all the business of the place is carried on. The sardine fishery, from June to November, occupies two-thirds of the population. From three to four hundred vessels are employed with five men to each boat. Calm weather is most favourable for fishing. The sardines are taken in large seine nets, one side floating with corks on the surface of the water, the other falling vertically. The sardines, attracted by the bait, try to force themselves through the meshes of the net, and are caught by their gills. The bait used is called "rogue:" the best is composed of the roe of the cod-fish, pounded and steeped in salt water for several days; sometimes the roe and flesh of the mackarel is used. Rogue is made in Norway and Denmark, but principally at Drontheim, and is very expensive, costing about sixpence the lb.; hence an inferior bait is substituted, composed of shrimps and other small crustacea, with fish salted, and the heads of anchovies, all pounded and putrified together. But this kind of decomposed bait is forbidden by the fishery laws. The employment of it accounts for the rareness of good sardines, as the remaining of such a substance in the body of the animal cannot fail of corrupting it. It is a pretty sight to behold the little fleet employed in the sardine fishery return in the evening, laden with the results of the day's work. The fish, when landed, are counted out into baskets, shaken in the water, and taken up to one of the curing-houses: of these there are about sixty in Concarneau. In the first shed we saw above fifty women employed in taking off their heads—" detêter " it is called—an operation they effect with great dexterity. With one cut at the back of the neck the head is separated and the fish " éventré " at the same time.

The sardines are next placed in little wire trays, with divisions like a double gridiron, and fried or dipped in boiling oil, an operation principally performed by the women of Pont l'Abbé, who are supposed, like the Germans of our baking and sugar-refining houses, to be peculiarly constituted to resist heat. The gridirons are then hung up to drain. The sardines are next packed in tin boxes, cold oil poured over them, and the boxes soldered down. From 800 to 900 boxes are placed in a boiler and boiled for half an hour to test the boxes, and those which leak are put aside. They are of English tin, and the making of them is the winter's occupation. Finally, the boxes are stamped with the name of the establishment, and packed in deal cases for exportation. The sardine is a very delicate fish, and easily decays. It is only taken out of the net with a rake (*raquette*); in summer, numbers

30.   Dolmen. Trégunc.

are spoiled from being heaped in the boats, and at whatever hour the boats come in the fish go through the whole process of curing, as they will not keep till the next day. Concarneau exports from 15,000 to 20,000 barrels of sardines annually.

Only a part are "anchoitée," that is, preserved like the anchovies of the Mediterranean, the others are salted in casks; and quantities, only slightly salted, are packed in baskets, to be sent to the provincial markets. It is estimated that twelve hundred million fish have been caught this year. The sardine fishery extends along the whole western coast of Brittany from Douarnenez to the Loire.

One of the curiosities of Concarneau is its aquarium, under the direction of M. Guillon. It consists of six cisterns, made by the blasting of the solid rock, and comprising an area of large extent, within a walled enclosure. In these cisterns the water is renewed at each turn of the tide through narrow openings in the wall. Three of these reservoirs are reserved for fish, the others for crustacea—lobsters and langoustes. Of these they keep from 10,000 to 15,000 at a time, and send them off daily, when fattened, to Paris and the principal markets of France. It was curious to see the dread shown by the common lobster to the langouste. They all were adhering to the sides of the reservoirs as if afraid to encounter their more powerful companions. Quantities of turbot, also reared for sale, were in one of the cisterns, darting with the greatest rapidity in the water when the keeper threw in pieces of sardines for them to eat. At the end of these cisterns is a building, with every arrangement for the culture of fishes—rows of little troughs, and other vessels, to contain them. Many of the fish are so tame, they came immediately to the keeper on his making a noise in the water with his fingers. Here are fish of every description, and naturalists

31.   Rocking Stone.   Trégunc.

have every facility of studying their habits. Among others, we saw the graceful little sea-horse or hippocampus, a native of the seas of Brittany as well as of the Mediterranean.

From Concarneau to Quimperlé is a distance of above eighteen miles. The road runs near the sea, over a large tract of land covered with furze (*ajonc*), which, in Brittany, grows from five to six feet high, forming a solid impenetrable mass. Huge blocks of granite are scattered about in every direction, jutting out out from among the furze—menhirs, cromlechs, and dolmens—a perfect wilderness of Celtic remains. We drove over an extent of several miles of furze-covered hills and heathy land. Before we reached the village of Trégunc we stopped to see a large dolmen on the side of the road, and further to the right a rocking-stone, twelve feet long and nine feet thick, standing about fifteen feet from the ground, the second largest in Brittany. It is poised by a little projection, like an inverted cone, upon another rock lying half-buried in the ground. The upper block can easily be set in motion by the hand. It is called by the country people "La pierre aux maris trompés," and was formerly consulted by husbands to test the fidelity of their wives. Even now the partner of a faithless wife is said to be incapable of giving to the stone the rocking motion it so easily receives from another.

On the left we passed the majestic ruins of the castle of Rustéphan, *i.e.* Run, mound, of Stephen, having been built by Stephen Count of Penthièvre at the beginning of the twelfth century. It belonged in the thirteenth to Blanche of Castile, the mother of St. Louis. The present edifice dates from the fifteenth. One of the sides remaining has a cylindrical tower with pinnacled doorway, and the windows have stone mullions.

32.   Château of Rustéphan.

Pursuing our road through blocks of granite, we descended into the valley of Pontaven, the town of millers, according to the old saying—

"Pont Aven, ville de renom;
Quatorze moulins, deux maisons;"

a little port built upon rocks, at the foot of two elevated mountains, over which are scattered masses of granite boulders, obstructing the course of the river which bounds over them. The banks are lined with woody slopes; wooden bridges cross the river at intervals; mills are established on the ledges of the rocks on its sides; and the noise of the mills, with that of the sparkling river tumbling through the rocks in waterfalls, keep up a perpetual din. Pontaven is celebrated for the quantity of its salmon: so much is taken, that it used to be said that the millers fattened their pigs upon this fish, which was literally true, as they took the small salmon, called glésils, in nets (*poches*) for that purpose. Salmon now is very dear. At the mouth of the Pontaven river was a castle, whose proprietor had the privilege of firing upon the fishing-boats which returned up the river without giving to the castellan their finest fish, which his steward went down to select. Pontaven is seven and a half miles from Bannalec, the nearest railway station. After remaining a few hours we drove on to Quimperlé—in Breton, Kemper (confluence) Ellé—so called, because it is at the confluence of two rivers, the Elle and Isole:—

"Vous reverrai-je encore, ô fleuve de l'Ellé,
Vous, Izôle, où mon cœur est toujours rappellé!
Les eaux sombres de l'Ellé, claire ceux de l'Izôle;
De ces bords enchantés je dirais chaque saule."

BRIZEUX.

Quimperlé is a great resort for fishing, the Quimperlé salmon and trout being renowned throughout Brittany, and even at Paris. This town is beautifully situated, surrounded by high hills, in a valley, watered by these bright rivers, the hills covered with gardens, orchards, the Ursuline, Capucine, and other convents, and crowned by the steeples of the Gothic church of St. Michael. Its principal building is the church of St. Croix, formerly that of a Benedictine abbey, celebrated for its riches. The island of Belle-Ile-en-Mer then belonged to it. It is a most singular edifice, built in the eleventh century, after the model of the church of the Holy Sepulchre at Jerusalem. In 1862 it fell down, but is at present in course of restoration, after its original plan. The old abbey buildings are now occupied by the Prefecture. We were given permission to pass through the convent garden—the workmen and building materials having blocked up the other entrances—to see the crypt in which is the tomb of Saint Gurloës, first abbot of Quimperlé. His effigy, with crosier in hand, his feet resting on a dragon, lies upon a monument, about three feet high, with an opening in the lower part. The saint—Saint Urlose, as the Bretons call him—is invoked principally for the gout, and persons so afflicted crawl through the hole under the tomb, where, suspended by chains, is an iron hook. They twist a lock of their hair round this hook, and tear it off with violence, hoping to propitiate the saint by this mortification—evidently a remnant of heathen times, when hair was sacrificed to deities or to the memory of departed friends.

At Quimperlé was buried John de Montfort, rival of Charles of Blois for the ducal crown. Sent to Paris under a safe-conduct by the Dauphin John, Philip of Valois had him shut up in the Louvre, whence he escaped, after a captivity of three years, to England. Edward III. espoused his cause and granted him some troops. After an unsuccessful attack upon Quimper, De Montfort died (1345) at Hennebont, and was buried in the church of the Dominicans at Quimperlé. He appointed Edward III. guardian of his son, and Edward immediately occupied Quimperlé and caused money to be struck in his name. Lord Lewis of Spain, on the side of Charles of Blois, made a descent upon Quimperlé at the head of 6000 men, and pillaged the whole country. On the news reaching Sir Walter Manny, he hastened to meet the enemy, took possession of their fleet, and made such carnage of the soldiers, that they were all killed or taken prisoners, and Lewis of Spain escaped with difficulty. The country about Quimperlé is beautiful—wood and water in every direction. The department of Finistère is traversed by three hundred streams, and has an extent of nearly four hundred miles of coast. We were advised to go and see the rood-screen of the chapel of Rosgrand, but had no time. We visited the ruins of the church of St. Columban. Above a round-arched doorway is a beautiful flamboyant window, between two canopied niches. We next walked up to the Place near St. Michel, where a cattle-market was being held. The Breton peasants, with their long shaggy uncombed hair hanging round their shoulders—they comb and wash only on fête days—their dirty canvas bragou bras, patched coats, and sabots with tufts of straw crammed in, looked more dirty than it is possible to imagine. Cleanliness is the last of the Breton virtues. The market and the fair are the two great events of the country, and people flock from great distances to sell their merchandise. But of all extraordinary animals is the Breton pig, as tall as a donkey; a lean, long-necked, ragged, bristly, savage-looking beast, as ill kept as its master, and it runs like a greyhound when approached. The Breton cow is very small, small as the Kerry cows of Ireland, very pretty and very productive. The Breton butter is proverbially good, and is given out most liberally, in lumps as big as loaves, at the tables-d'hôte. It is brought to market in jars which the women carry upon their heads. It is to the Queen-Duchess that Brittany, and indeed all France, owes the privilege of eating butter in Lent. It was forbidden as animal food by the laws of the Church, and oil, a vegetable production, ordered as a substitute. In 1491, Anne solicited of Rome, for herself and household, permission to eat butter on fast-days, alleging, as a plea, that Brittany did not produce oil. Encouraged by this favour, Brittany obtained the same indulgence, and it was acquired successively by the other provinces of France; but all are originally indebted for the privilege to the good Queen-Duchess Anne.

Next day, leaving the department of Finistère, we entered that of Morbihan, and went by rail to Lorient on the river Scorff, here joined by the Blavet. It was formerly the seat of the French East India Company; it is now one of the five military ports of France and the residence of a maritime Prefect. In the Place Bisson is the statue of a young officer of the French navy, a native of Guemené-sur-Scorff (Morbihan). When commanding, in 1827, a brig in the Greek Archipelago, he was attacked by two pirate vessels. Nine out of his fifteen men were killed and himself wounded; the enemy crowded on the deck. Desiring the survivors of his crew to jump overboard, " Now," cried he to the pilot, " is the moment for revenge!" and, setting fire to the powder-magazine, he blew up himself, his ship, and the pirates who had boarded her. Next morning the bodies of seventy Greeks lay on the sea-shore, showing the success of his self-devotion. The pilot, who, with four sailors, was saved, received the decoration of the Legion of Honour. On the pedestal of Bisson's statue is an inscription, concluding with these words: "Mort en héros, pour son roi et sa patrie, ses amis le pleurent, la France le regrette, et ses frères d'armes envient son sort."

From here we proceeded to Hennebont (Breton, "old bridge"), famous, in the War of Succession, for its heroic defence by Jeanne de Flandre, during the captivity of her husband, Jean de Montfort, who had been taken prisoner at Nantes and carried off to Paris. Jeanne, who, as Froissart says, had the courage of a man and the heart of a lion, placed herself at the head of his party. Like another Maria Theresa, she presented herself before the Breton lords, with her infant son in her arms, and received their oaths of allegiance. She then joined in the defence of Hennebont, which was invested by Charles of Blois. Clothed in armour and mounted on a war-horse, she galloped up and down the streets, encouraging the inhabitants. She ordered the ladies of her suite and other women of the place to cut short their "keytels," carry the stones to the ramparts, and transport pots of quick-lime to throw down upon the enemy. At the head of 300 horsemen, the Countess, who rode better than any squire, sallied out of the town, attacked and burnt the enemy's camp, retreated to Auray, and, a few days after, re-entered Hennebont, with banners flying and trumpets sounding. But the blockade was so close that provisions were wanting, and the garrison compelled her to agree to a capitulation, unless within three days assistance arrived from England. The time was on the point of expiring, and a herald had approached the gate of the city to receive the keys in the name of Charles of Blois, when the Countess, from her window, perceived at sunrise the English fleet entering the port in full sail. She exclaimed, "We are saved!" The siege was raised, and the Countess, says Froissart, kissed Sir Walter Manny and all his companions, one after the other, two or three times, like a noble and valiant dame. "Better," observed Charles, when he heard the news, "that Jeanne, instead of her lord, had been shut up in the Louvre." He left the carrying on of the siege to Lewis of Spain, and proceeded to Vannes and Auray. Some fragments of walls are all that remain of Jeanne de Montfort's castle, which was situated on a height on the other side of the river in the "Vieille ville." The town on the left bank of the Blavet is called the "Ville neuve" and the "Ville close," being surrounded by walls. Large vessels ascend the Blavet to Hennebont. It is traversed by a light and elegant railway viaduct of twelve arches. We saw on the quay a quantity of red iron-ore from Bilbao.

Hennebont is a very pretty town; the principal building is the church of Notre Dame-de-Paradis, of the sixteenth century, with a fine square stone tower, surmounted by a beautiful spire, and a tall porch, forming one side of the tower. This handsome church has lately been restored. The scenery about the Blavet is very pretty—the banks wooded, and fertile fields. We took a boat and rowed up the river, passing the ruined Abbaye de la Joie, where a hideous château has been built. This was a Cistercian convent, founded in the thirteenth century by Blanche of Navarre, wife of Duke John I. (*le Roux*). The chapel of Notre Dame-de-Paradis formerly belonged to the convent; but when the parish church was demolished, the Abbey ceded this chapel to the town, reserving the privilege of a separate seat for the Abbess, who, on the Sunday after St. John's day, had her crosier carried before her in state by one of her vassals at high mass and vespers.

From Hennebont we went by rail to Auray, and established ourselves for some time in the Pavillon d'en Haut, a most comfortable hotel. Auray is situated on the slope of a hill, the streets narrow and steep.

Our first drive was to Ste. Anne d'Auray, one of the most famous places of pilgrimage in Brittany, on account of its miraculous well and church. It has been called the Mecca of Brittany. Here, according to the legend in the seventeenth century, Ste. Anne appeared to a countryman, and directed him to dig in a certain field, where he would find her image, and to build a chapel there. Guided by a miraculous light, Nicolazic discovered the statue, and erected a chapel on the site.

The spring where Ste. Anne first appeared is now enclosed in a large basin of cut stone. Near it is the church, in course of reconstruction. It stands in a

33.   Scala Sancta. Ste. Anne d'Auray.

court surrounded by covered galleries for the shelter of the pilgrims. Two flights of steps, called the Scala Sancta (after that of St. John Lateran), lead to a platform over the three entrance gates, upon which is an altar surmounted by a cupola, where mass can be heard by 20,000 persons. The steps are ascended by the pilgrims barefooted, as they do at Rome. The fête of Ste. Anne is celebrated on the 26th of July, when pilgrims arrive from all parts of Brittany to visit the miraculous statue, to ascend the holy staircase, and to drink or wash in the sacred fountain. It was a fête day when we visited Ste. Anne. There was a large assemblage of people, and booths were erected round the court, where were sold rosaries and the wire brooches, with scarlet and blue tufts of worsted, called *épinglettes*, worn by the Bretons in their hats as a token of their having made a pilgrimage. We saw exhibited the photograph of a young lady, said to have lately recovered from paralysis after bathing in the holy well. So world-wide is the fame of Ste. Anne d'Auray that a traveller mentions having seen at her shrine an embroidered altar-cloth of Irish damask, with "Irlande: Reconnaissance à Sainte Anne, 1850," woven into the pattern. The convent, with its enclosure, the Scala Sancta, fountain, and miraculous bush, all date from the seventeenth century. There is a railway station for Ste. Anne, within two miles of the church.

Returning to Auray, we went to the Chartreuse, which owes its origin to the chapel of Saint Michel-du-Champ founded (1382) by John de Montfort, afterwards Duke John IV., on the spot where, in 1364, he gained the battle of Auray, which obtained for him the duchy of Brittany. The chapel is close to the railway station. In the fifteenth century it was given to the Chartreux, and became a monastery of the order which existed until the

Revolution. The present church was built at the end of the reign of Louis XV.

The battle was fought on the marshy plain by the side of the muddy river Alrée. It is fully described by Froissart. In the two armies were assembled all the chivalry of England, France and Brittany. The Breton-English were commanded by Sir John Chandos; the French, by Du Guesclin; with de Montfort were also Sir Robert Knollys, Sir Hugh Calverley and Olivier de Clisson; with Charles of Blois, Du Guesclin, the Comte d'Auxerre, the Viscomtes of Rohan and Tournemine, and Charles de Dinan. At the moment of the battle, the white greyhound of Charles of Blois deserted his master and ran to his rival de Montfort, who was on horseback, and caressed him, standing on his hind paws. De Montfort recognised the dog by his collar, ornamented with the arms of Brittany, and this incident passed through his army as a favourable omen. The dog was known to have been the gift of a witch to Duke John the Good, who bequeathed it to his niece Jeanne, wife of Charles of Blois.

Both armies heard mass, confessed themselves, and received the Communion before they opened the battle. The war cry of Charles was, "In the name of God and St. Ives," Montfort repeated the motto of his family, "Malo mori quam fœdari" (better to die than be sullied), and his troops advanced to the onset to the cry of "Malo." Both chiefs wore the ermines emblazoned on their armour and their standards; and relatives and friends were ranged in battle array against each other. Following the tactics which had been successful at Cressy and Poitiers, Chandos quietly awaited the impetuous attack of the Franco-Breton army, which was unable to shake their antagonists, who returned the charge. The melée was fearful, but the battle was in favour of the English. Charles performed prodigies of valour. In vain Rohan and Laval rallied round him with the flower of the Breton knights; the prince was a prisoner, and an English soldier despatched him by plunging a dagger into his throat. Du Guesclin sustained all the force of the fight with his heavy steel mace, his battle-axe and his sword; but his mace was broken, the handle of his axe carried away, his sword shivered, and he had no other weapon left but his gauntlets, and was nearly overpowered by numbers, when Chandos, who fought with a battle-axe, entreated him to surrender, "Messire Bertrand, rendez-vous, cette journée n'est pas vôtre; il faut céder à la fortune, une autre fois vous serez plus heureux." Convinced of the truth of Chandos' words, Du Guesclin surrendered to him the handle of his sword. Beaumanoir was among the prisoners; and Clisson, who never left the field, lost an eye in the conflict.

A hair shirt was found, with thick knotted cords round the waist, upon the body of Charles, for he delighted in deeds of mortification. He often used to place pebbles in his shoes, and once walked two leagues barefoot in the snow to visit the relics of St. Ives, in consequence of which he was laid up for three months. He was buried at Guingamp, and his widow and children desired his canonisation; but de Montfort, fearing such a step would render him unpopular in Brittany, persuaded Pope Gregory XI. to refuse it.

Du Guesclin, after he recovered his liberty, was destined, three years later, to be a second time the prisoner of the English at Navarrete, when the Black Prince replaced on his throne the cruel, perfidious Don Pedro. When Sir Hugh Calverley asked for the freedom of Du Guesclin, he was met by the reply, "Il ne faut pas lâcher ce dogue de Bretagne, si fatal aux Anglais." It was represented to the Black Prince that report ascribed his detention to fear or jealousy; upon which he sent for Du Guesclin, who told him he was tired of listening to the squeaking of the mice in his prison, and longed to hear the nightingales of Brittany. He named his own ransom at 100,000 florins, the Black Prince reduced it to 60,000; and the Princess of Wales contributed 20,000. It was paid by Charles V. "Had it been ten millions," says his biographer,

"France would have paid it all." In the Musée des Archives at Paris is preserved an order of Charles V. to his treasurer, to prepare 30,000 Spanish doublons, to be paid to the Prince of Wales for the ransom of Du Guesclin, adding, "il touche notre honneur grandement." This is the most ancient royal autograph in the collection. Charles calls him Bertran de Caclin. The Constable, in a deed of gift of the Château of Cachant to the Duke of Anjou, signs "Bertrain."

A school for deaf and dumb occupies the Chartreuse, directed by the Sœurs de la Sagesse. We were shown round by a deaf and dumb guide, who made us write on his slate what we could not explain on our fingers, and he also wrote his reply. He showed us a series of paintings, copies of Le Sœur's Life of St. Bruno in the Louvre, which are said to have been executed by the monks of the Chartreuse. Attached to the church is a sepulchral chapel containing the bones of the victims of the unfortunate descent on Quiberon, when the immense armament of French royalists who were landed in British ships, perished. They were commanded by d'Hervilly, an old officer of the Constitutional Guard of Louis XVI., and he had for lieutenant Count Charles de Sombreuil, whose sister had rendered the name illustrious by her heroism in the Reign of Terror. They landed at Carnac, where Georges Cadoudal and a band of Chouans awaited their arrival. Hoche, at the head of a republican army, hastened to meet them. Every thing depended upon their rapidity of action, but three days were lost in disputes about the command among the emigrant generals. They took possession of the peninsula of Quiberon, a strip of land about six miles long by three wide, united to the mainland by a narrow tongue of sand a league in extent, called the Falaise. Fort Penthièvre, placed on the plateau of a steep rock, and bathed on each side by the sea between the peninsula and the Falaise, defends the approach by land. The emigrant army was protected by the English fleet which lay in the bay of Quiberon, one of the safest and most sheltered on the coast. The defence of Fort Penthièvre was entrusted to some republican soldiers taken from the English prisons. In a night encounter d'Hervilly was killed. Hoche marched upon Fort Penthièvre, which was given up to him by the traitor soldiers. La Puisaye threw himself into a boat and gained the English fleet. The emigrant army was thrown into the greatest disorder; the "Bleus," as the republican soldiers were called, pressed close upon them, and Sombreuil, driven to the water's edge, and deserted by his troops, offered to capitulate, on the condition that the lives should be spared of all save himself. "Yes," cried the republicans with one voice. They demanded that the fire of the English corvette should cease, and there being no boat at hand, Gesril du Papeu swam to the English ship, and having delivered his message, returned and surrendered himself prisoner. It is said that Hoche considered the capitulation sacred, but Tallien arrived armed with full powers from the Convention to treat the emigrants according to law. The prisoners had been conducted to Auray; Hoche, unwilling to be the witness of acts he could not prevent, returned to Brest. Not one French officer would consent to be a member of the military commission who were to try, or rather condemn, the captives. It was composed of Belgians and Swiss, and it was difficult to induce the soldiers to execute the sentence. Sombreuil and a few others were shot at Vannes. The execution of the rest took place in a field now called the Champ des Martyrs. They were brought out in twenties, and placed before a trench, dug beforehand, and shot. The massacre lasted three weeks. In all there were 952 victims. Two chapels have been erected; the one attached to the Chartreuse, and the other on the Champ des Martyrs. That in the Chartreuse has inscribed over the front, in letters of gold, "France in tears has raised it." The interior walls are overlaid with black and white marble, with two marble bas-reliefs by David of Angers: one representing the Duc d'Angoulême praying over the bones of the victims in 1814, when they were transferred from the Champ des Martyrs to the Chartreuse; the other, the laying of the first stone of the mausoleum by the Duchesse d'Augoulême in 1823. In 1829 the solemn inauguration of the expiatory monument took place; and it must have been touching to the spectators to have assisted at the ceremony with the Duchesse d'Augoulême, daughter of Louis XVI. and Marie Antoinette, niece of the martyr saint the Princess Elizabeth, and herself long subjected to imprisonment and indignities. Only one year after this ceremony she again took the road to exile, where she ended her troublous life, a pattern of piety and resignation—

"Sa mort fut le soir d'un beau jour."

In the centre of the mausoleum is the vault containing the bones, and over it a sarcophagus on a pedestal, upon which are inscribed the names of the victims. On the sarcophagus are busts of Sombreuil and the other chiefs of the expedition; and a profile of Monseigneur d'Hercé, Bishop of Dol, one of the victims. Of the bas-reliefs on the mausoleum, one represents the heroic act of Gesril du Papeu, with the words " I hoped in God, and shall not be afraid;" the other, the landing of the emigrants on the shore of Carnac, with " All my brothers are dead for Israel;"—these inscriptions are all in Latin. Others are round the monument:—" Unworthily slain for God and the King;"—" Precious before God is the blood of his saints;"—" For our lives and our laws;"—" You will receive a greater glory and an eternal name." Our deaf and dumb guide let a light down into the vault to show us the bones of the victims, collected in one common sepulchre. The Chartreuse convent therefore commemorates two great tragedies of history: in ancient times the battle of Auray, which caused the death of Charles of Blois, the captivity of Du Guesclin, and the slaughter of the flower of Breton chivalry by the swords of their fellow Bretons. In modern days, the massacre of the royalists at Quiberon—both the horrible consequence of civil war.

We then repaired to the " Champ des Martyrs," where took place the execution of the royalists. At the end of an avenue of silver firs is the expiatory chapel, with a granite portico, in the Doric style. Above is inscribed, " It is here they fell," and " The memory of the just shall be eternal."

On the tomb is written, " Tombeau des royalistes courageux defenseurs de l'autel et du trône, ils tombèrent martyrs de leurs nobles efforts. Quel Français pénetré des droits de la couronne ignore ce qu'il doit à ces illustres morts."

The inn Pavillon d'en Haut is particularly comfortable and reasonable, and the people very obliging. Wishing to taste the crêpes we had seen before, they procured some, and gave them to us hot—we thought they resembled a greasy crumpet.

34.   Champ des Martyrs. Auray.

Auray is a good central point for visiting the Celtic remains :—menhirs, dolmens, cromlechs, all of which are as plentiful here as are calvaries, shrines, and churches in Léon. They seem all concentrated on these dreary wild landes, sometimes covered with furze bushes, at others strewn along the coast.

Next day we drove to Locmariaker, nine miles from Auray, through Crach. On the right is the river or estuary of that name; over which a bridge is contemplated at La Trinité, to communicate with Carnac. Locmariaker is at the extremity of the peninsula formed by the rivers of Crach and Auray, at the entrance of the Morbihan. It must have been a place of some importance in the time of the Roman occupation of Gaul, as there are the remains of a circus, whose walls now enclose the cemetery, of a Gallo-Roman house, with baths, frescoed walls, and marble pavement. We picked up some fragments of Roman bricks which lie strewn upon the ground in great abundance. Midst these Roman remains are gigantic menhirs, barrows, and dolmens, vestiges of a still more ancient race. Locmariaker has two large tumuli, both vast tombs.

We first visited the Manné-er-Hroëk, the Montagne de la Fée, or de la Femme, which bears in the marine charts the name of "Butte de César," for it was the fashion with antiquaries to attribute to Cæsar and the Romans every Celtic monument, although bearing no resemblance whatever to any work of these conquerors. The Montagne de la Fée is a galgal or tumulus of elliptic form, about thirty feet high, formed of dry stones. It was opened in 1863, and found to contain a sepulchral chamber or dolmen, outside of which lay a granite stone above three feet long, inscribed with various figures, and, in the middle, a cartouche, with hatchet-shaped characters. There were also found a number of celts (stone hatchets or knives), a green jasper necklace, and some glass beads, which have been transferred to the museum at Vannes. The guide who furnished the light and showed us the grotto is the widow of a Polish officer. She had a Scotch terrier, which she wanted us to accept. The legend of the mound is this:—A widow had the misfortune of losing her only solace, her son, compelled by law to embark for foreign lands. Years rolled by; he did not return. All said he was lost; but the heart of a mother hopes for ever, and the sad Armorican went every day to the point of Kerpenhir, whence she surveyed the ocean, and searched the depths of the horizon with tearful eyes for the purple sail[1] which was to bring joy and peace to her dwelling. One day, when she was returning sad as

35. Sculptured Stone. Manné er Hroëck. Locmariaker.

---

[1] The sailors of the Morbihan cover their sails with a substance which makes them of a dark red colour.

usual to her desolate home, she was accosted by an old woman, who enquired the cause of her troubles; and, on hearing them, advised her to heap a pile of stones, so that, mounting on the summit, she might see to a greater distance, and perhaps discern the long looked-for vessel. During the whole night the two women worked, and carried in their aprons the stones they gathered on the heath. In the morning their task was finished, and the Bretonne was scared to see the enormous heap that had been piled together; but the other quieted her fears, and helped her to climb to the top, whence soon the happy mother beheld the vessel of her son. The fairy, her assistant, had disappeared. This story evidently bears a vague tradition of this tumulus having been raised by a woman, and of some maritime expedition made by him for whom it was probably destined. The name of fairy is attached in Brittany to everything—mountains, springs, grottoes, rocks; every accident in nature is explained by a fairy origin.

The next object we saw is also attributed to the fairies, the great menhir, called Men-er-Groách, or stone of the fairies. It is the largest menhir known, but it has been broken into three pieces, some say by thunder. Put together, it measures about 67 feet in length, and is 16 feet in diameter. The wonder is how it was placed there, for it is little less than the obelisk of St. Peter's, which took 800 to 900 men and 70 horses nearly a year to raise,—a work which was the great triumph of Fontana the engineer. The menhir is estimated to be one-third the height of Notre Dame at Paris.

Lying also prostrate on the ground, by the side of it, is a smaller menhir, which is, however, above 30 feet long.

Close to these gigantic menhirs is the large dolmen (Breton, *daul,* table, and *mœn,* stone), known as the "Table de César," or the "Dol des Marchands." We walked under it to see the curious hatchet-shaped figure sculptured on one of the upper stones. The common belief is that these dolmens or table-stones were Druidic altars, and the guides will show you the furrows for the blood of the human sacrifice to run down; but human bones having been found under some of these dolmens, lead one to suppose they were tombs. In the Scandinavian countries the peasants call them "Giants' Graves."

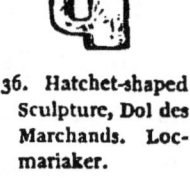

36. Hatchet-shaped Sculpture, Dol des Marchands. Locmariaker.

The other great tumulus of Locmariaker is the Mont Heleu or Manné-Lud, also opened in 1863, and supposed to have been the sepulchre of a number of persons, perhaps of a whole generation. It has, like the Montagne de la Feé, a galleried chamber or dolmen, the floor formed of an enormous slab across the centre, on which is a sculpture resembling a celt; other sculptured stones were found in the same chamber. At the other end of the dolmen was an avenue of stones, some supporting the skeletons of horses' heads. This tumulus was probably the tomb of some great warrior: the horses' skeletons were the remains of a sacrifice, and the human bones of beings who had been immolated to accompany the earthly remains of their great chief to another world.

We took a boat for Gavr' Inis, or the Goat Island, and embarked on the Morbihan (Breton, Little Sea), an inland sea, that gives its name to the department. Shut out from the ocean by the two peninsulas of Locmariaker and Rhuys, which form a narrow gully between the points of Kerpenhir and Port Navalo, this sea contains an archipelago of islands, numbering, according to tradition, as many as the days in the year. Of these, the Ile aux Moines is the largest. The arms of the sea forming the rivers of Auray and Vannes run into it. The navigation of the Morbihan is very dangerous, the ocean entering it by this narrow opening in three distinct currents; it is an endless labyrinth of rocks and water; its granite shores, torn by the sea, are indented with creeks, capes, and inlets.

Gavr' Inis is a small island, surmounted by a tumulus, which forms a conspicuous object, seen from all the mounds and dolmens around. It is a galgal of

37.   Entrance to the Tumulus of Gavr' Inis.

heaped stones, in the centre of which is a dolmen or galleried chamber, which was opened in 1832, and is the most curious monument in the Morbihan. The gallery, with its square sepulchral chamber at the end, is above fifty feet long and about five wide, composed of two rows of granite menhirs, or upright stones, which form the sides, with horizontal stones resting on them, ending in a chamber consisting of eight menhirs, with an enormous slab, thirteen feet long, placed over them horizontally to form the roof, and another, nearly as large, to form the floor. These stones are of granite, and no cement is used to unite them. They are covered with incised figures of unknown meaning: sculptures in concentric whorls or circles, as if tattoed like the cheek of a New Zealander; and the only forms to be distinguished are serpent-like figures, and the representation of an axe, similar to those to be seen in the Grotte des Fées, the Dol des Marchands, and the Manné-Lud. In one of the side stones of the chamber are two handle-looking projections, with a

38.   Sculptured Stones.   Gavr' Inis.   39.

recess behind, said, probably erroneously, to be the place where the victims were bound. No celts or other objects of antiquity were found in the grotto, which must have been previously rifled of its contents. These sculptures cannot have been executed without the use of metal instruments. There are also Celtic remains in the Ile aux Moines and other islands of the Morbihan, but our guide did not encourage us to extend our sail to visit them. The current between the island and Port Navalo is sometimes of great rapidity and violence.

Next day we went to Carnac to see its marvellous avenues of menhirs. The Celtic remains here are of a different character from those of Locmariaker. Here there is quantity, at Locmariaker size. The monuments of the last are covered with strange characters and signs; in Carnac they are all plain and silent, according to the laws of the Druids, who prohibited writing, in the fear of thereby divulging their mysteries, and also that the people might not neglect to cultivate their memories.

> " Tout cela eut un sens, et traduisit
> Une pensée ; mais la clé de ce mystère,
> Où est elle ? et qui pourrait dire aujourd'hui
> Si jamais elle se retrouvera ? "—CAYAT DELANDRE.

Before reaching Carnac, we stopped at Kermario on the left, and got out of the carriage to inspect the army of large menhirs about the windmill. They are arranged in eleven rows, some sixteen feet high, placed with the small end in the ground. They are all of a sombre grey, many of them clothed with straggling lichens of various species.

This wild heathy tract was covered with the blue flower of the dwarf gentian, and strewed all over with menhirs. Before arriving at Carnac, the road passes the avenues of Menec, all running in the same direction as those of Kermario, from east to west: among these are some of the largest stones. The third large group, at Erdevan, we saw on our way from Carnac back to Auray by another road.

> "D'un passé sans mémoire incertaines reliques,
> Mystères d'un vieux monde en mystères écrits."
> LAMARTINE.

We do not pretend to enter into the various explanations attempted of this wonderful monument. The legend at Carnac is, that St. Cornély, pursued by an army of pagans, fled towards the sea; finding no boat at hand, and on the point of being taken, he transformed the soldiers into stones.

> "Les soldats de deux rois idolâtres
> Poursuivaient notre saint déjà l'ami des pâtres,
> Et sur un chariot traîné par de grands bœufs
> Le bons vieux Cornéli se sauvait devant eux;
> Or, voici que la mer, terrible aussi l'arrête;
> Alors, le saint prélat, du haut de sa charrette
> Tend la main : les soldats, tels qu'ils étaient rangés,
> En autant de menhirs, voyez! furent changés.
> Telle est notre croyance, et personne n'ignore
> Que le patron des bœufs c'est ici qu'on l'honore;
> Aux lieux où la charrette et le saint ont passés,
> Le froment pousse encor plus vert et plus pressé."
> BRIZEUX.

St. Cornély is the patron of bullocks. When a

beast is ill, his owner buys an image of St. Cornély, and hangs it up in the stable till its recovery. In the church of Carnac is a series of fresco paintings portraying the principal events of his life, and outside, a sculpture representing him between two bullocks. The head of St. Cornély is preserved here; the pulpit is of forged iron, and in the sacristy is shown a silver gilt monstrance of the Louis XIV. period, with a representation of the Supper at Emmaus, chased in relief round the foot. We walked to the Mont St. Michel, a tumulus of stones with sepulchral dolmen, opened in 1862, but now closed. It was found to contain objects of the "Stone" age, a number of jade celts from four to sixteen inches long, some perforated beads and pendents for a necklace, and there were traces of burnt bones. Like most monuments of Celtic origin, these tumuli were regarded with religious veneration; and the first teachers of Christianity, to enlist the old worship to the cause of truth, marked each of these monuments with the symbol of the new faith. Thus the cross was placed on the menhir, and a chapel built upon Mont St. Michel, and, as we have before seen, on Mont Dol, and other high places of Druidic worship. The little chapel dedicated to St. Michel, which surmounts the tumulus, forms a conspicuous landmark from every point, and commands a most extensive view over the stones of Carnac ranged in their eleven lines, on a treeless plain, the Morbihan, and the long dreary peninsula of Quiberon.

Returning by another route, we alighted at the inn at Plouharnel to see a collection of jade celts, gold torques, and necklaces of beads, found in the neighbourhood, belonging to the landlord, M. Bail, who has them all arranged in a frame. They were discovered in a group of dolmens near the village, opened in 1830, consisting of three grottos or allées couvertes, a kind of triple dolmen, covered over with a mound. The central grotto and gallery had been opened before. The second dolmen had also a grotto or allée couverte, in which was found an earthen pot, containing ashes and three gold necklaces. In the third were some fragments of pottery. Three gold necklaces, composed each of a single plate of metal, an inch and a half wide, with fragments of the earthen vessels in which they were found, together with stone celts and some pieces of bronze, extracted from the dolmen, we afterwards saw exhibited in the "Musée du Travail" of the Universal Exhibition of 1867. These dolmens belong to a much later period of civilisation than those of Locmariaker—to the "Bronze" Age.

The number of dolmens in the Morbihan is estimated at 250. In the department of Finistère they are set at double the number. All are supposed to have been originally covered with earth. The bodies are more frequently buried than burnt. The dolmens contain implements of stone and bone, occasionally gold and bronze, but never iron. To judge from the comparative quantities found in the different departments, it may be assumed that they are the work of people who have entered France from the west, and have gradually worked their way by the rivers and valleys further up the country. In this secluded spot we found a large English family located, ten in number; they had been living there several months. Before reaching Erdeven, at Kerserho, on a large lande or heathy plain, we arrived at another series of the great Carnac army of stones, of which they are a continuation. They are arranged in nine parallel rows, as may be clearly distinguished by standing upon one of the stones; but the lines are rather interrupted by hedges and ditches. Some are menhirs planted vertically on the end, others enormous blocks simply laid upon the soil. They extend half a league from north to south, more numerous than Carnac, but generally not so tall, the highest from ten to twelve feet, but very large. The road is strewed with Druidic monuments. At Corcorro, between Plouharnel and Erdeven, on a farm, a short distance off the road, is a dolmen, the largest in the Morbihan. Its original length appears to have been 45 feet; the part preserved is 24 feet by 12 feet wide, and is covered with two slabs: one of these is enormous, about six feet wide. It is used as a cart-shed, and, when we saw it, contained bundles of hemp and a hemp-breaker. One of the top stones overhangs the others, showing the dolmen to have been originally larger. A number of ragged

40.   Dolmen of Corcorro.

children clustered upon the top, as if they had been accustomed to group themselves for a picture. They effectually prevented any of us sketching the dolmen, for, as soon as we began to draw, they all, in number about forty, came down from their height and pressed closely around us. From Auray we took a carriage to Vannes, a tidal port, one league from the gulf of Morbihan, and capital of that department.

Its people, the Veneti, were the head of the Armorican confederation, and commanded the fleet in time of war. Their vessels had sails of prepared skins, their cables were chains of iron. They traded with the Scilly Islands, and brought back tin, copper, skins, slaves, and dogs, objects of traffic with other nations. The Armorican confederation made a vigorous resistance against Cæsar, who sent round for the Roman fleet and beat them in a naval battle in the Morbihan sea. The Romans had attached to their ships large sharp scythes which mowed down masts and rigging, and a dead calm rendering the enemy's ships immovable, they were soon taken, burnt, or sunk. This battle ended the war with the maritime states of the west. Cæsar showed little mercy to the conquered: all the senators were put to death, and the rest of the population sold by auction to furnish the slave-markets of Italy.

We walked to the promenade, called the "Garenne," where Sombreuil, Renée de Hercé, bishop of Dol, and twenty-two others of the emigrants, were shot. Sombreuil was about twenty-six or twenty-seven years of age, a native of Périgord. He always persisted in the same account of the capitulation. His last words were :—" Si j'avais pu imaginer que des militaires pussent manquer à leur parole donnée sur le champ de bataille, je n'aurais jamais consenti à une capitulation; elle me cause des regrets amers qui me suivront jusqu'au tombeau. Adieu, Messieurs, nous trouverons justice et clémence devant un tribunal où la fraude des hommes ne saurait jamais parvenir." A republican officer offered to bandage his eyes: "Non," he exclaimed, "je veux voir mon ennemi jusqu'au dernier instant." Requested to kneel, Sombreuil answered: "Je le veux bien; mais je fais observer que je mets un genou pour mon Dieu, et l'autre pour mon roi." Thus ended the most illfated expedition that history has ever had to record.

The cathedral of Vannes has a richly-sculptured north porch of Kersanton stone, and another, facing the Rue des Trois Duchesses. Also, a Renaissance chapel, called the Chapelle du Saint Sacrament or du Pardon, with a hideous roof replacing the original. Adjoining are the remains of the elegant cloisters of the cathedral, with basket-handled arcades of the fifteenth century. In the cathedral is also the chapel of St. Vincent Ferrier, the great preacher of the fifteenth century, whose labours extended over almost every country of Europe—Italy, Germany, France, Switzerland, and Great Britain. San Vicente Ferrar, a Dominican monk, was the son of an attorney, originally of Valencia, in Spain, of which city he is the tutelar saint. In Spain he led the way in preaching a crusade against the Jews and Moors, who were persecuted by the Inquisition with the most cruel bigotry. Invited to Brittany by Duke John V., he fixed himself at Vannes, where, after having evangelised the province, he died in 1419. He was buried in the cathedral. The Duchess Jeanne de France, daughter of Charles VI., was present at his deathbed, and insisted on laying him out. By her own desire, she was buried at his feet. Philip II., King of Spain, desired his relics, but did not succeed in obtaining them. The little house in which St. Vincent Ferrier lived is preserved (No. 13, Rue des Orfèvres). A tiny room, up a narrow staircase, is now converted into a chapel, in which are shown the stone which served him as a pillow, his lamp, and other relics.

The Maison du Parlement or Château Gaillau is a curious old building, with its entrance by a stone staircase and turret. Vannes was the usual residence of Dukes John IV. and V., and had formerly three châteaux: La Motte, of which the Hôtel de la Préfecture occupies the site; Plaisance, half a mile out of the town, where Duke Francis I. died; and La Hermine, scene of John IV.'s treacherous imprisonment of the Constable Clisson, which was razed in 1614. It had two towers—one demolished in 1770, the other still standing, called the "Tour du Connétable," because it was within its walls he imprisoned Clisson.

The Duke had resolved on his death, to prevent the marriage of Clisson's daughter Marguerite to Jean de Bretagne, Count de Penthièvre, son of Charles of Blois.[1] The story is well related by d'Argentré.

The Duke of Brittany summoned his barons and knights to a council at Vannes, and entertained them in the Castle de la Motte. He behaved in the most friendly manner, and invited the Constable, the Lords of Laval and de Beaumanoir, to see the castle of Hermine he was building. He led the Constable by the hand through the chambers, and when they arrived at the keep, said, " Sir Oliver, there's not a man who understands masonry so well as yourself; enter and examine the walls well, and if you say it is properly built, it shall remain." The unsuspecting Constable ascended the staircase, when the door was closed upon him and he was seized and loaded with three pairs of fetters. The Duke ordered him to be put into a sack, his hands and feet tied, and to be

---

[1] Jean and his brother were twenty-eight years in captivity in England. The King offered them their liberty, if they would acknowledge him as their suzerain lord; but they would not buy their freedom at the expense of their allegiance to the King of France, who had always been the friend of their house. His brother died in prison: Jean was ransomed through the medium of Robert de Vere, Duke of Ireland, by the Constable Clisson, that he might marry his daughter; but he only exchanged his captivity to pass the remainder of his days in wars against his suzerain, to gratify the ambition and resentments of his wife.

thrown secretly at night into the sea. But the Constable owed his life to the loyalty of Jean Bazvalen, who, like another Hubert, did not obey his master's commands, the laws of his sovereign being less sacred in his eyes than the dictates of humanity and honour. Clisson was set at liberty, on agreeing to pay 100,000 livres and to surrender the town of Jugon and some other fortresses. This perfidious attempt occasioned a war of three years, and was retaliated by Clisson's daughter and grandsons upon Duke John V.

The Tour du Connétable, which formed the northeast angle of the Château de la Hermine, is now used as a museum of Celtic antiquities, and contains various objects collected in the tumuli of the Morbihan. We observed one very large jade celt, eighteen inches long, found, we understood, in the Butte de Tumiac. At Vannes the States of Brittany held their sittings, and here took place the union of that province with France, 1532.

About twelve miles from Vannes is Korn-er-hoët, demesne of the Princess Baciocchi, cousin of the Emperor. It was formerly surrounded by woods and the interminable lande of Lanvaux, which stretches its desolate length along the Morbihan from Baud to Rochefort. This district had been, from time immemorial, the abode of some eighty families of gipsies, who lived there in clay huts under the rule of a chieftain. The sight of this barren wilderness had so impressed the Princess Baciocchi, in a tour she made in Brittany in the year 1857, that she obtained the sanction of the Emperor to reclaim it. She caused a temporary châlet to be built for her occupation at Kern-er-hoët, and, superintending the works herself, in a few years effected a wonderful transformation. A model village has been formed, with church and schools, a well-ordered agricultural population organised, farm-buildings erected, roads macadamised, the barren lande drained and reclaimed, and the château surrounded by a well-wooded park.

Great attention has been paid to the details of the dairy farm; all the disposable milk is made into Dutch cheese. The cows are those of Brittany and Ayrshire; the pigs from England. The whole demesne comprises about 1300 acres, and the benevolent Princess resides entirely on the scene of her labours, among the people whose condition she has so ameliorated.[1]

From Vannes we made an excursion into the peninsula of Rhuys, on the south of the Morbihan Sea. We first stopped at Sarzeau, where Lesage, the amiable author of 'Gil Blas,' was born, of whom it was written on his epitaph:—

> "S'il ne fut pas ami de la fortune,
> Il fut toujours ami de la vertu."

Then on to the ducal fortress of Sucinio, situated

---

[1] The Princess is since dead.

on the borders of the ocean. It is a magnificent ruin, built in 1250, by Duke Jean le Roux, to deposit his treasures, in case an invasion of the French should compel him to leave his duchy. The position is well chosen, its situation on the sea-shore enabling him easily to embark his treasures.

This formidable "coffre fort" was a favourite residence of the Dukes of Brittany, who came here as a relief from the cares and ceremonies of a Court. Its name, of which Sucinio is a corruption, Soucy-ny-ot, synonymous with the Sans-Souci of the great Frederick, shows its intention. This locality was long celebrated for its fine air, and its peaceful character. Louis XIV. used to say to his courtiers—

> "Désirez vous un pays de repos et de délices?
> Allez habiter l'île de Rhuys."

Partly demolished, Sucinio presents a mass of now only picturesque ruins, a curious type of the architecture of the thirteenth century. Five of the eight enormous battlemented towers remain, and the flamboyant window of the chapel on the upper floor of the building is still preserved. Traces of the portcullis and drawbridge are visible. Over the gallery is an escutcheon, with a couchant lion holding the arms of Brittany, between two stags, also couchant, at the foot of a tree. The sea that bathed the walls of the castle has been driven back by the accumulation of mud and the crumbling of the walls.

Here was born Arthur III., Comte de Richemont, Constable of France, and afterwards Duke of Brittany. This illustrious man, equally great as a warrior and politician, does not take his merited place in the page of history, owing probably to the partiality of French historians, who were always jealous of the glory of Brittany. Except Du Guesclin, no other constable has rendered greater service to France.

A prisoner at Agincourt, where he commanded the van, he fought with the Maid of Orleans,[1] at Beaugeney, took Talbot captive at Patai, reconquered almost the whole of Normandy, entered Paris in 1436, and finally expelled the English by the crushing victory of Formigny, having staked his honour to drive them out of the kingdom.

---

[1] Jeanne had at first a great aversion to Richemont, as he ridiculed the idea of the army being commanded by a woman. Dunois effected a reconciliation. Richemont said to the maid—" Jeanne, on me dit que vous voulez me combattre. Je ne sais pas si vous êtes de par Dieu ou non : si vous êtes de par Dieu, je ne vous crains en rien ; si vous êtes de par le Diable, je vous crains encore moins." It was through her mediation he became reconciled to the King (1429). Two years afterwards she was executed.

Seven years after, he succeeded to the ducal crown; but such was the confidence of Charles VII. in his loyalty, that he retained the supreme command of the French army with his new dignity. He reigned only fourteen months. Richmont always caused two swords to be carried before him when he appeared in presence of the King; a naked sword, as Duke of Brittany, and the other sheathed and the point turned downwards, as Constable of France. The title of Earl of Richmond, styled by the French Comte de Richmont, dates from the Conqueror. Alan Rufus, son of the Earl of Brittany, accompanied Duke William to England, and commanded the rear of the army at the battle of Hastings. For these services, he was rewarded with the hand of the Conqueror's daughter, and all that northern part of Yorkshire, now called Richmondshire, where he built, on the river Swale, the town and castle of Richmond. The title passed through Alice, daughter of Constance of Brittany, to Pierre de Dreux, and descended through him to all the Dukes of his house, until John IV., having gone over to the King of France, was deprived of the earldom by Act of Parliament, in the reign of King Richard II.; but Henry IV. again conferred the title upon his stepson Arthur, afterwards the celebrated Constable and Duke of Brittany.

We returned to breakfast at Sarzeau; then on to the Abbey of St. Gildas de Rhuys, founded on this inaccessible coast by St. Gildas, an English saint, the schoolfellow and friend of St. Samson of Dol and St. Pol de Léon, and which counted among its monks our Saxon St. Dunstan, who, carried by pirates from his native isle, settled on the desolate shores of Brittany, and became, under the name of St. Goustan, the patron of mariners.

St. Gildas built his abbey on the edge of a high rocky promontory, the site of an ancient Roman encampment, called Grand Mont, facing the shore, where the sea has formed numerous caverns in its rocks. They are composed chiefly of quartz, and are covered to a great height with innumerable small mussels. The tide was too high to admit of our entering into any of the grottoes, but the piles of dark rocks beaten into every form by the violence of the waves, rising sometimes to the height of sixty feet, are very imposing. St. Gildas, in the twelfth century, had Abelard for superior, who, on his appointment, made over to Eloise the celebrated abbey he had founded at Nogent, near Troyes, which he called the Paraclete or Comforter, because he there found comfort and refreshment after his troubles, but his peace soon ended on his arrival in Brittany. His gentle nature was unable to contend against these coarse, ferocious, unruly, Breton monks. As he writes in his well-known letter to Eloise, setting forth his griefs :—

"J'habite un pays barbare, dont la langue m'est inconnue et en horreur : je n'ai de commerce qu'avec des peuples féroces ; mes promenades sont les bords inaccessibles d'une mer agitée ; mes moines n'ont d'autre règle que n'en point avoir. Je voudrais que vous vissiez ma maison, vous ne la prendriez jamais pour une abbaye : les portes ne sont ornées que de pieds de biche, de loups et d'ours, de sangliers, des dépouilles hideuses des hiboux. J'éprouve chaque jour de nouveaux périls ; je crois à tout moment voir sur ma tête un glaive suspendu."

But if Abelard hated the monks, they equally detested him, and one day tried to poison him, but he escaped through a gate in the garden wall, still pointed out, to the sea shore, where his friend and protector, the Count de Rhuys, awaited him in a boat.

The abbey is now in the occupation of twelve sisters of the "Charité de St. Louis," who have a school for poor girls, and, in the summer, take in families to board who come here for the benefit of the bracing air of this fine wild coast. There is a kind of establishment for bathing in the little bay below the abbey. The board and lodging is moderate, three francs and a half a day, wine, tea, and sugar, not included. Boys are admitted up to thirteen, but the men are sent into the town.

Part of the abbey church is Romanesque : a semi-circular choir, with three round chapels and the transepts. The nave and tower are of modern date. The pavement is covered with tumulary stones. Four children of Duke John III. le Roux are buried here, and one of Joan of Navarre and John IV. In the Treasury are several pieces of plate, among which is a Renaissance chalice, with six canopied statuettes of Apostles forming the knop; and a cross of the same period, a châsse of St. Gildas, his head and arm both encased in silver reliquaries. His tomb is in the church. Encrusted in the wall outside the church are the figures of two knights on horseback in mailed armour, conical Norman helmets, long pointed shields, and lances in the attitude of combat. The church and convent of St. Gildas belonged to the family of Bisson, whose self-devotion is commemorated by a statue at Lorient. He passed here many years of his early life, and wishing to preserve the buildings from ruin, gave them as a present to the parish. St. Gildas is called by the Bretons St. Feltas. There is a rude coloured print in the church relative to the legend of Comorre, or Comor, the Breton "Blue Beard," in which St. Gildas plays a conspicuous part. The story, as told by Emile Souvestre, is this:—Guerech, Count of Vannes, the country of white corn, had a daughter, Triphyna, whom he tenderly loved. One day, ambassadors arrived from Comorre, a Prince of Cornouaille, the country of the black corn, demanding her in marriage. Now this caused great distress, for Comorre was a giant, and one of the wickedest of men, held in awe by every one for his cruelty. As a boy, when he went out, his mother used to ring a bell to warn people of his approach. He shot a child in order to prove his gun; and, when unsuccessful in the chase, would set his dogs on the peasants to tear them in pieces. But most horrible of all, he had had four wives, who all died one after the other, under suspicion of having been killed by either the knife, fire, water, or poison. The Count of Vannes, therefore, dismissed the ambassadors, and advanced to meet Comorre, who was approaching with a powerful army; but St. Gildas went into her oratory, and begged Triphyna would save bloodshed, and consent to the marriage. He gave her a silver ring, which would warn her of any intended evil, by turning, at the approach of danger, as black as the crow's wing. The marriage took place with great rejoicings. The first day six thousand guests were invited; on the next as many poor were fed, the bride and the bridegroom serving at table, a napkin under their arms. For some time, all went on well. Comorre's nature seemed changed, his prisons were empty, his gibbets untenanted; but Triphyna felt no confidence, and every day went to pray at the tombs of his four wives. At this time there was an assembly at Rennes of the

Breton Princes, which Comorre was obliged to attend. Before his departure, he gave Triphyna the keys, desiring her to amuse herself in his absence. After five months he unexpectedly returned, and found her occupied in trimming an infant's cap with gold lace. On seeing the cap, Comorre turned pale; and when Triphyna joyfully announced to him that in two months he would be a father, he drew back in a rage and rushed out of the apartment. Triphyna saw that her ring had turned black, which betokened danger, she knew not why. She descended into the chapel to pray; when she rose to depart it was midnight, and she saw the four tombs of Comorre's wives open slowly, and they all issued forth in their winding-sheets. Half dead with fear, Triphyna tried to escape; but the spectres cried, "Take care, poor lost one! Comorre seeks to kill you." "I," says the Countess, "what evil have I done?"—"You have told him that you will soon become a mother; and, through the Spirit of Evil, he knows that his child will kill him, and that is why he has murdered us, when we told him what he has just learned from you." "What hope then of escape remains for me," cried Triphyna."—" Go back to your father," answered the phantoms." "But how escape when Comorre's dog guards the court?"—"Give him this poison which killed me," said the first wife." "But how can I descend this high wall?"—"By means of this cord which strangled me," answered the second wife." "But who will guide me through the dark?"—"The fire which burnt me," replied the third wife." "And how can I make so long a journey?" returned Triphyna."—"Take this stick which broke my skull," rejoined the fourth spectre. Armed with these weapons, Triphyna sets out, silences the dog, scales the wall, sees her way through the darkness, and proceeds on her road to Vannes. On awakening next morning, Comorre finds his wife fled, and pursues her on horseback. The poor fugitive, seeing her ring turn black, turned off the road and hid herself till night in the cabin of a shepherd, where was only an old magpie in a cage at the door. Comorre, who had given up the pursuit, was returning home that road, when he heard the magpie trying to imitate her complaints, and calling out "Poor Triphyna!" he therefore knew his wife had passed that way, and set his dog on the track. Meanwhile, Triphyna felt she could proceed no further, and laid down on the ground, where she brought into the world a boy of marvellous beauty. As she clasped him to her arms, she saw over her head a falcon with a golden collar, which she recognised as her father's. The bird came to her call, and giving it the warning ring of St. Gildas, she told it to fly with it to her father. The bird obeyed and flew with it like lightning to Vannes; but, almost at the same instant, Comorre arrived; having parted with her warning ring, Triphyna, who had no notice of his approach, had only time to conceal her babe in the cavity of a tree, when Comorre threw himself upon his unhappy wife, and with one blow severed her head from her body. When the falcon arrived at Vannes, he found the King at dinner with St. Gildas; he let the ring fall into the silver cup of his master, who recognising it, exclaimed, "My daughter is in danger; saddle the horses, and let St. Gildas accompany us." Following the falcon, they soon reached the spot where Triphyna lay dead. After they had all knelt in prayer, St. Gildas said to the corpse, "Arise, take thy head and thy child, and follow us." The dead body obeyed, the bewildered troop followed; but, gallop as fast as they could, the headless body was always in front, carrying the babe in her left hand, and her pale head in the right. In this manner, they reached the castle of Comorre. "Count," says St. Gildas, "I bring back your wife such as your wickedness has made her, and thy child such as Heaven has given it thee. Wilt thou receive them under thy roof?" Comorre was silent. The Saint three times repeated the question, but no voice returned an answer. Then St. Gildas took the new-born infant from its mother, and placed it on the ground. The child marched alone to the edge of the moat, and picking up a handful of earth, and throwing it against the castle, exclaimed, "Let the Trinity execute judgment." At the same instant the towers shook and fell with a great crash; the walls yawned open and the castle sunk, burying Comorre and all his fellow partners in crime. St. Gildas then replaced Triphyna's head upon her shoulders, laid his hands upon her, and restored her to life, to the great joy of her father.—Such is the history of Triphyna and Comorre.

On our way back to Vannes we saw on our left the Butte de Tumiac, or Butte d'Arzon, the largest tumulus of the Morbihan. It was opened in 1853, and found to enclose a chamber full of pulverised bones and various curious objects. From Vannes we also visited the stately castle of Elven, about four miles from the station of that name; not built on a lofty site, for, in the fifteenth century, the barons had descended from their heights to places more convenient of access, and where water was more easily obtained. The Breton feudal lords of Rohan, Rieux, Clisson, and Penthièvre, no longer required fortified places as means of defence against the French and English, but, in consequence of their own internal divisions, to defend them in their wars with their duke or among themselves. The castle of Elven is situated in an insulated coppice wood, in the midst of the lande of Elven. It was the chief place of the lordship of l'Argoët (in Breton, "upon the wood"), and is also called the fortress of Largoët.

41.   Castle of Elven.

The ruins, which occupy a large enclosure, consist chiefly of two towers; the principal one, 130 feet high, is octagonal; the other, which is not above 100 feet in height, is split from top to bottom. The battlemented walls are nearly 20 feet thick at the base. A wide deep moat surrounded the castle, and it was furnished with subterranean passages and everything requisite to make it a model of the military architecture of the fifteenth century. The donjon has two granite staircases; one leads to the top, whence may be seen Vannes and the Morbihan, with its islands. Here, in 1793, the Royalists established signals. In the castle of Elven, Henry of Richmond, then only fifteen, with his uncle, Jasper Tudor, Earl of Pembroke, were detained by Duke Francis II. for fifteen years. Fugitives after Tewkesbury, they were thrown by a tempest upon the shores of Brittany. Henry was claimed both by King Edward IV. and Louis XI., and was kept by Duke Francis as a pledge of the good faith of Edward towards Brittany. Perhaps also Francis may have entertained some ill-feeling towards Henry from his bearing the title of Earl of Richmond, which had been held for more than three hundred years by the Dukes of Brittany. Francis revived the claim to the title which Henry VI. had conferred (1452) on Edward Tudor, father of Henry. Subsequently, on the assurance of the King of England that he only required the release of Henry to invest him with the Order of the Garter and to give him his daughter, the Princess Elizabeth, in marriage, Duke Francis made over the Prince to the English Ambassador, and he was about to embark at St. Malo for England, when the Duke's Grand Treasurer (Landais) arrived, warned Henry of his danger, and helped him to take refuge in the sanctuary of the church, whence he afterwards withdrew him again to place him in honourable captivity for twelve more years, till King Edward's death. A party being formed in England, aided by the Duchess of Brittany, Françoise de Foix, Henry attempted a descent; but the plan being discovered, after seeing the English coast, Henry was obliged to return to Brittany and his ships were scattered in a storm. Again within his power, Landais listened to the offers of King Richard III., and agreed to give him up; but Henry, informed in time, left Vannes, threw himself into the forest, and escaped to France, where he obtained from the regent, Anne de Beaujeu, the assistance which enabled him to mount the English throne.

The castle of Elven, with those of Rieux and Rochefort, belonged to the Maréchal de Rieux. Elven was rebuilt by him with the materials of the old; but they were all dismantled by the orders of the Duchess Anne in 1496, to punish her guardian for his revolt. Yet Rieux acted as he thought best for the welfare of his late master and his daughter, whose cause he defended against the interested views of the King of France. Rieux had that keen sense of honour which is one of the characteristics of the

Breton gentleman. When he reproached Anne de Beaujeu, regent, to her brother Charles VIII., for having instigated the King to attack Nantes, contrary to his engagements, Anne replied, "He had no written promise." "Et quoi, Madame!" he indignantly exclaimed; "la parole d'un roy, ne vaut elle pas mille scellez?" Louis de Rieux, the last of the race, was shot on the Champs des Martyrs. True to the motto of his house, "A toute heure, Rieux," he showed himself ready "at any hour" to die for the altar and the throne.

Elven is the scene of M. Octave Feuillet's "Roman d'un jeune Homme pauvre;" and the keeper who shows the ruins points out the spot whence the "Hero of Romance" took the leap to prove his loyalty, and which gained him the hand of the lady.

Next morning we started early by rail to Questembert, to meet the diligence for Ploërmel, twenty miles from this station, passing through Malestroit. We saw quantities of chestnuts on our road, and were told they were largely exported to England. They come principally from the neighbourhood of Redon and other places in the department of Ile-et-Vilaine, where they grow as abundantly as described by Madame de Sevigné, when writing from the Château des Roches, in the same department: "Pour nous, ce sont des châtaignes qui font notre ornement. J'en avois l'autre jour trois au quatre paniers autour de moi. J'en fis bouillir, j'en fis rôtir, j'en mis dans mes poches, on en sert dans les plats, on marche dessus, c'est la Bretagne dans son triomphe."

Ploërmel derives its name (plo-ermel, land or territory of Armel) from an anchorite of the sixth century, who treated a dragon which ravaged the country in the time of King Childebert in the same manner as St. Pol de Léon disposed of the monster at Batz.

The façade of the church of Saint Armel has a number of grotesque carvings—the sow playing the bagpipes, the cobbler sewing up the mouth of his wife, &c.; but it is principally remarkable for its eight painted windows of the sixteenth century, lately restored, and the monumental effigies of two Dukes of Brittany; the one, John II., who was killed at Lyons, where he went to settle some differences with his clergy, on the occasion of the coronation of Pope Clement V. A wall, loaded with spectators, fell, and the Duke was crushed in its ruins; the Pope escaped with being only thrown from his mule.

The other effigy is that of Duke John III., or the Good, whose death was the signal for the War of Succession. He died at Caen. These tombs were formerly in the Carmelite convent founded by John II., who, on his return from the Holy Land, established the first Carmelite convent in Brittany, and brought monks from Mount Carmel to inhabit it.

The tombs were destroyed in the Revolution, but the two statues were saved. They are of white marble, and are placed on a monumental slab, side by side, with this inscription: " De tous temps la fidélité Bretonne rendit hommage à ses souverains." Duke John II. is represented in a hauberk of mail, the hood turned back, with cotte d'armes, shield, and sword. Duke John III. has his head encircled by the ducal crown, his hair long, his genouillières, cuissarts, &c., of plate armour. His shield and cotte d'armes are semé of ermines, and by his side is the dagger of miséricorde, which served to kill the fallen enemy unless he cried for mercy. When James II. passed through Ploërmel after the Battle of the Boyne, a fugitive and a dethroned monarch, the Carmelite monks would not take him in; but he found in the little village of Penfra the hospitality they had refused him. Here is an establishment, directed by a brother of Lamennais, the celebrated author of 'Paroles d'un Croyant,' where people of all nations—Indians, negroes from Senegambia, and others—are educated and taught trades of every kind, and sent back to their own countries.

The people about Ploërmel and Josselin speak French instead of Breton, the prevailing language of the Morbihan department. It is nearly seven miles between Ploërmel and Josselin. Equally distant from each, at Mi-voie, in the centre of a star formed by avenues of firs and cypresses, is an obelisk set up to commemorate the famous " Combat des Trente,"

42.　　　　Column of the Thirty.

which took place on this spot in 1351, and on which are inscribed the names of the thirty who fought on the French side. It was during that period of the War of Succession when hostilities were carried on by the two Jeannes, Marshal Beaumanoir, the Breton commander of the garrison of Josselin for Jeanne de Penthièvre, gave a challenge to Bembro', as he is called, the English captain who held Ploërmel for Jeanne de Montfort and her infant son, in consequence of an alleged infraction by the latter of a truce, agreed upon between the Kings of France and England, in which it had been stipulated that the peasants and those not bearing arms should be unmolested. In spite of this compact, the English soldiers devastated the country and committed every kind of excess. Jean de Beaumanoir repaired to Ploërmel to remonstrate, and it was agreed to settle the dispute by a fight between thirty warriors from each camp. The prophecies of Merlin were consulted, and found to promise victory to the English. The appointed place of meeting was by a large oak, the "Chêne de Mi-Voie," on a lande or large plain, half way from each town. The battle began with great fury, at first to the disadvantage of the Bretons, when Bembro' was killed, which threw dismay among the English; but a German, who succeeded in the command, rallied their courage, and the melée became thicker than ever. Beaumanoir was wounded, and his loss of blood and his long fast produced a burning thirst, and he asked for water. "Bois ton sang, Beaumanoir, ta soif se passera," was the reply of Geoffroy du Bois; and Beaumanoir, forgetting his thirst and his wound, continued the fight. The

English kept their ranks close, till Guillaume de Montauban broke them by a stratagem and threw them into confusion. He mounted his horse and pretended to fly, then suddenly turned upon the English with such force that he threw seven down and broke their ranks:—

> "Grande fut la bataille et longuement dura :
> Et le chapple (carnage) horrible est deçà et delà ;
> La chaleur fut moult grande, chacun si tressua (sua) ;
> De sœur et de sang la terre rosoya (rougit).
> A ce bon samedi Beaumanoir si jeuna ;
> Grand soif eut le baron, à boire demanda ;
> Messire Geoffrey du Bois tantôt répondu a :
> 'Bois ton sang, Beaumanoir, la soif te passera ;
> Ce jour aurons honneur, chacun si gagnera
> Vaillante renommée, ja blâme ne sera.'—
> Beaumanoir le vaillant adonc s'évertua,
> Tel deuil eut et telle ire que la soif lui passa ;
> Et d'un côté et d'autre le chapple commença :
> Morts furent ou blessés, guères n'en échappa."—BRIZEUX.

Sir Robert Knollys, Sir Hugh Calverly Croquart, and others were made prisoners, and thus ended the Battle of the Thirty; gained, however, in a most disloyal manner, Montauban getting the aid of a horse, when all the other combatants fought on foot.

The Breton knights returned to Josselin, their helmets decorated with branches of the broom—

> "In every basnet a bright broom flower;"

the place where the battle was fought running, according to the French poem,

> "Le long d'une génetaie qui était verte et belle."

Josselin is celebrated for its château, where died, 1407, Olivier du Clisson, the contemporary and brother of arms of Du Guesclin, whom he succeeded in the dignity of Constable of France, which no one for some time would accept, not thinking themselves worthy of replacing him. Both differed widely in position and character. Du Guesclin, though of a noble family, had not the advantage of fortune like Clisson, who had immense wealth and landed possessions, which made him a kind of sovereign in the duchy. He willed away a million of money. Clisson was a statesman, Du Guesclin's sole glory was in arms. Clisson was cruel, intriguing, and insatiable for riches; Du Guesclin was humane, loyal, and disinterested. Both were equal in bravery and physical force: the lance of Du Guesclin and the axe of Clisson[1] carried all before them. Clisson joined with Du Guesclin in freeing the country from the "Great Companies," and his most celebrated action was the defeat of the Flemings at Rosbecq. Few subjects have been so powerful, or have filled so important a part, as Olivier du Clisson. He was true to his sovereign after his reconciliation, and to

---

[1] "Olivier du Clisson dans la battelle va
  Et tenant une martel qu'à ses deux mains porta,
  Tout ainsi qu'un boucher abbatit et versa."
    MS. CHRONICLES OF BERTRAND DU GUESCLIN.

his children after him. John IV. had scarce closed his eyes when the daughter of Clisson, wife of Jean de Penthièvre, came to her father and said, "It depends only on you that my husband receives the inheritance of Brittany." "How?" asked the Constable. "By your ridding yourself of the children of De Montfort." "Ah! cruel and perverse woman," exclaimed Clisson; "if you live long, you will destroy the honour and property of your children;" and he accompanied his words with such violent menaces, that, seized with affright, she fled from his presence, and falling down, broke her thigh. The prophecy of Clisson was fulfilled, as we shall later relate. The ancient château in which he died was destroyed by Henry IV.; the present building was raised by Alain IX., Vicomte de Rohan, through Alain VIII., who married Beatrix, eldest daughter of the Constable, by which Josselin descended to the Rohans,[1] a house yielding to none in antiquity and illustration, being descended from the ancient sovereigns of Brittany, and allied with all the crowned heads of Europe,—" Princes of Bretagne" they were styled. But the Rohan family became unpopular in the duchy, when John II. attached himself to

---

[1] Their name is said to be derived from—Roh-yan-Rock-John, from a cadet of the family, who built his fortress on a rock.

Louis XI. and France, for the bribe of 8000 livres to himself and 4000 to his wife.

At the battle of St. Aubin du Cormier, which sealed the fate of Brittany, the Vicomte du Rohan betrayed his brother-in-law Duke Francis and the national cause, and fought on the side of France. He afterwards marched at the head of the French troops, and besieged Guingamp, where its brave defenders declared, "As long as there is a duchess in Brittany, we will not give up her towns." But they took Pontrieux and Concarneau, and in 1491 the Vicomte du Rohan was appointed by Charles VIII. Lieutenant-General in Lower Brittany. He was called by his countrymen the "Felon Prince;" and so detested was he and his race, that it passed into a proverb to say of a mean, treacherous, dishonest person, "Il mange à l'auge comme Rohan,"—"He eats at the manger (that is, the table of the King of France) like Rohan." "Un peu de jactance," therefore, justly observes Daru, in the proud motto of the Rohans:—

> "Roi ne puis,
> Prince ne daigne,
> Rohan je suis."[1]

The château of Josselin stands by a river, on which side it presents piles of towers and fortifications

---

[1] This, with "À Plus" and "Plaisance," were the Rohan mottoes previous to 1789.

covered with slate, a severe specimen of military architecture; while on the other side, the cour d'honneur, we see one of the handsomest châteaux of the Renaissance yet remaining in Brittany. This façade is richly ornamented with sculptures of varied and fanciful design. Immense gurgoyles, in the

43.   Château of Josselin.

form of serpents, stretching from the roof to the base, pierced ballustrades or galleries of lace-like delicacy, in which are introduced, according to the fashion of the period, the initial letters of the Vicomte Alain, A and V interlaced. The old Rohan motto, "À plus," and the escutcheon of gules, nine mascles or lozenges, occur in every part of this gorgeous front, and also on the finely-carved chimneypiece of the reception room (salle d'honneur). The whole of the château is in course of restoration by the Prince de Léon.

In the church of Josselin is the tomb of the Constable Clisson, with that of Marguerite de Rohan his wife; both statues were mutilated in the Revolution, but are now restored: they are of white marble on a black slab. Clisson is in armour, Marguerite has her hair plaited and confined in a network of pearls; she wears a long robe, with a surcoat above, furred with ermine. The motto, " Pour ce qu'il me plest (plait)," is in an oratory which belonged to Clisson, expressing his haughty and overbearing will. This same motto appears on his seal, affixed to a letter preserved in the archives of the empire, and he is recorded to have had it inscribed upon his Constable's sword, which, like Du Guesclin, he always wore unsheathed, to show he was ready at all times to fight the enemies of the crown.

There hangs in the church a picture of the finding of the image Notre Dame-du-Roncier, of which we relate the legend:—

Long before Josselin was a town, a poor labourer had remarked, on the spot where now stands the church of Notre Dame, a bramble bush, which the frost and snow of the roughest winters never deprived of its leaves, but it always remained fresh and green. Surprised at this strange phenomenon, he dug the soil under the bramble, and discovered a wooden statue of the Virgin. A marvellous light played round the head of the image. The man carried it home; but next morning, to his surprise, he found the statue under the same bush whence he had taken it. The miracle was repeated several times, and soon attracted crowds of devotees. A chapel was built to deposit the sacred image, houses followed next, and a little town gradually formed, which the Comte de Porhoët surrounded with walls, and Josselin, his son, endowed with his name, 1030. Such was the rise of Josselin. A celebrated pilgrimage still exists to Josselin on Whit Tuesday, resorted to by crowds of "aboyeuses" or barkers, people possessed with this kind of epilepsy, said to be hereditary in several families, and which is accounted for from the circumstance of a party of washerwomen having refused a glass of water to the Vierge du Ronçier, who went to them disguised in the garb of a beggar. The merciless creatures set their dogs upon the pretended mendicant, and thus brought down upon themselves and their posterity this fearful malediction. The disease is supposed to return periodically about Whitsuntide, and only to leave the afflicted when they are carried forcibly to the sanctuary of Notre Dame to press with their foaming lips the fragments still remaining of the ancient miraculous statue which was burnt upon the public Place in the time of the French Revolution.

We left Ploërmel at four o'clock in the morning for Montfort-sur-Mer, passing through Plélan; while the horses baited at a little auberge we got some hot coffee, and found a good fire in the kitchen. The landlady, shut in her "lit clos," did not disturb herself, but occasionally put out her head to give directions for our breakfast. On the left of the road is the forest of Paimpont, which formerly extended from Montfort to Rostrenan, a kind of neutral desert land, called Brocéliande, and famous, under that name, in the history of King Arthur. It was the theatre of the fairies' most wondrous enchantments. Here was the fountain of Youth and also that of Barenton, where they came every day to draw water in an emerald basin. Here, too, the enchanted Merlin has lain sleeping for centuries, enthralled by his pupil the fairy Viviana, who has cast a spell upon her master she knows not how to break.

Montfort, where we joined the railway, is celebrated for the legend of the duck and its ducklings, and was the residence of the De Montfort family until Guy Comte de Laval and Sire de Montfort married Françoise de Dinan, widow of the unfortunate Gilles de Bretagne, when the Montforts left their paternal demesne for the châteaux of Laval, Vitré, and Châteaubriant.

The railway took us to Rennes, an uninteresting modern French town, the old town was burnt down in 1720, and straight streets have risen up, with no traces of its having been once the ancient capital of Brittany. Indeed, so French is it altogether, that the saying runs—"Bon Breton de Vannes, bon Français de Rennes." It was here that Constance, heiress of the duchy, held her court, with Geoffrey Plantagenet, who, with their unfortunate son Arthur, were the only Plantagenets, dukes of Brittany. On the murder of Arthur, his sister Alice carried the ducal crown to her husband, Pierre de Dreux (called Mauclerc, from his animosity to the clergy), and from them descended the dukes of Brittany down to Queen Anne, whose double marriage conveyed the duchy to France and the Valois.

When Henry IV. made his solemn entry into Rennes, the Governor presented him with the three silver-gilt keys of the city, of rich workmanship; upon which the King observed, " Elles étaient belles, mais qu'il aimait mieux les clefs des cœurs des habitants."

The following year we made a tour along the banks of the Loire, and at Angers embarked on board the steamer for Nantes. The scenery down the Loire is rich, and the hills covered with vineyards, islands planted with willows, and sunny villages, or occasionally a gloomy fortress comes to view. Ingrandes is the frontier town, half in Anjou and half in Brittany, between the modern departments of Loire Inférieure and Maine-et-Loire. Lower down is St. Florent (Maine-et-Loire), with its recollections of the wonderful passage of the Loire by the Vendean army, so graphically related by Madame de la Rochejacquelin, and near the island of Meilleraie, where their brave General Bonchamps expired, after the fatal engagement of Chollet; his last act being the saving the lives of four thousand prisoners shut up in the church, and about to be executed by the exasperated Vendeans. "Grâce aux prisonniers" were his dying words. Opposite St. Florent is Varades, where the Vendeans landed after crossing the Loire. Only a feeble post opposed them. Had the republicans lost less time, and sent a force after their victory at Chollet, much calamity would have been spared to Brittany, and the Royalists themselves would have been saved the terrible defeats of Le Mans and Savenay.

Passing Ancenis, which rises in an amphitheatre on the vine-clothed hills, and, with its suspension-bridge, is one of the most picturesque points in the river, we reached Oudon, with its tall octagonal tower; on the left, in the department of Maine-et-Loire, nearly opposite, stands the ruined castle or

Champtoceaux, where Duke John V. was kept a prisoner by the implacable enemies of his house, the Penthièvre family.

Marguerite de Clisson, widow of Jean de Bretagne, Comte de Penthièvre, lived in retirement in her stately fortress of Champtoceaux, with her three sons, Oliver, Count of Blois, and his brothers. Marguerite inherited the pride, hatred, and cruelty, of her father, without his chivalrous loyalty and magnanimity. The kingdom was filled with troubles, and she thought it a favourable moment for reviving the pretensions of her family. John V. held his court at Nantes. She sent Oliver there to assure the Duke that his mother and brother were ready to do him homage; and he swore, on his own part, "de le servir envers et contre tous ceux qui peuvent vivre et mourir." John, delighted, made the young man share his bed, and treated him with the greatest distinction. Oliver expressed his regret that the age and infirmities of his mother prevented her going to court, and timidly insinuated the honour she would feel at a visit from the Duke. The Duke consented, and, sending off his plate to Champtoceaux, started with his brother-in-law, Count Oliver, and his attendants. Having passed the little river which separates Anjou from Brittany, they saw a man throwing the planks of the bridge into the water, and thus preventing the Duke's suite from following.

At the same time, Charles de Penthièvre, Margaret's second son, issued suddenly from a wood with an escort of lances and surrounded the Duke. There was no kind of indignity they did not make him suffer. He was tied upon his horse like a criminal, and conducted first to Clisson, Oliver leading him with a halter round his neck. The Penthièvres, who would not let the place be guessed where they held their captive, conducted him at night, sometimes on foot, from fortress to fortress, from dungeon to dungeon; at the same time circulating the report that they had drowned him in the Loire. As a last insult, they took him to Champtoceaux, where Marguerite visited him in prison to exult over his misfortunes. Meantime the Breton barons, indignant at the treason of which their Sovereign was the victim, raised an army for his deliverance, and civil war broke out with redoubled fury. His heroic wife, Jeanne de France, showed an untiring energy to save him. Undaunted by the threats of the Penthièvres,—who sent word to her, if she did not desist from hostilities they would cut her husband in pieces, nor by the messages from the Duke himself assuring her that her zeal would cost him his life,— she induced her brother, the Dauphin, to order the Penthièvres not to attempt the life of their prisoner; she besieged, one after the other, all their castles, and at last compelled Marguerite to capitulate to save her own life. Finding herself and family in a perilous position, Marguerite agreed that the Duke should be released (he was at Clisson), and that she and her sons should retire where they wished, on their promise to appear at the summons of the Breton nobles. Immediately on his liberation, Duke John ordered the destruction of Champtoceaux. A parliament assembled at Vannes in 1424, condemned Marguerite and her sons to capital punishment, and declared all the Penthièvre possessions to be forfeited to the State. But the culprits had all escaped the kingdom, except the youngest son, William, a child only ten years of age, who had been given as a hostage for the appearance of his mother and brothers, and was condemned to languish for twenty-seven years in prison, where he lost his eyesight—a victim to crimes in which he had not been an accomplice. John had made a vow, during his detention, to give, if he regained his liberty, to the church of Notre Dame at Nantes, his weight in gold; and most conscientiously did he perform his promise, for we read, "He placed himself in his war armour in the balance, and caused the opposite scale to be filled with gold till it had attained the weight of the first; that is to say, three hundred and eighty marks, seven ounces"—which sum was delivered over to the church. Vows of this nature are not unfrequently recorded. When Don Carlos, the ill-fated son of Philip II., lay ill, he vowed to give to the Virgin, on his recovery, four times his weight in gold plate, and seven times his weight in silver. The vow was fulfilled; but the Prince was placed in the scale in a damask robe and fur coat, and weighed only seventy-six pounds—so much was he reduced by his long illness.

Nantes is a cheerful, busy, handsome city, but wanting in the picturesque characteristics of the towns of Lower Brittany. Quimper, Vannes, Rennes, and Nantes, have all been successively capitals of the duchy, but Nantes was the usual residence of its dukes.

The cathedral contains its principal artistic monument, the tomb of Duke Francis II. and his second wife, Marguerite de Foix, called "sein de lys," from the beauty of her complexion. It was erected by their daughter, the Queen-Duchess Anne, and was executed by Michel Colomb, a sculptor of St. Pol de Léon, originally a herd-boy. This monument, considered a masterpiece of the Renaissance, is not copied from any Italian original, but is entirely the offspring of the artist's own fancy. There is much simplicity in its design and execution. The tomb, about five feet high, is of white marble, diapered with ermine and the letter F. On a black slab repose the effigies of the Duke and Duchess, and at their feet are lying a lion and a greyhound, holding their several escutcheons. Four large allegorical figures are at each angle of the tomb, representing the cardinal virtues. Justice carries the book of the laws, and the sword by which she makes them respected. This figure is said to be the portrait of the Duchess Anne. Temperance, in a monastic dress, is characterised by a bit and a lantern. Prudence, double faced, holds a mirror and a compass, and has a serpent at her feet. This figure is in the costume of a peasant girl of St. Pol; the second face, that of an old man, is also in the dress of Lower Brittany. Strength or Fortitude, handsome, resolute, and calm, strangles a dragon with his grasp.

Upon the principal sides of the tomb are the twelve Apostles, and below, in niches, sixteen mourners (pleureuses) in monastic habits, the faces and hands white, the rest of the body black. The beautiful attitude of these figures is much admired. Some are kneeling, others are seated—all in the attitude and expression of prayer. This monument was originally in the church of the Carmelites, whence it was transferred to the cathedral.

Besides the remains of Duke Francis and his two wives, it formerly contained the heart of his daughter, the Queen-Duchess Anne, enshrined in a golden case in the form of a heart, surmounted by a crown, and surrounded by a cordelière; but the tomb was rifled during the Reign of Terror. It now holds the remains of the Constable Duke Arthur III.

Duke John IV. also died at Nantes, after his long eventful reign, having acquired a military glory which earned him the name of Conqueror, and equalled that of Du Guesclin and Clisson. Twice he lost and twice he regained his crown. He alienated Du Guesclin and his faithful subjects by his partiality to England. The Bretons rose, and he fled to Edward III.; but when Charles V. entered the duchy, with the intention of confiscating it to the crown of France, the Bretons all united to defend their nationality against the ambition of the French King, and recalled their Sovereign. So great was the enthusiasm on his arrival at St. Malo, that the nobles plunged into the water to approach his ship; and even the widow of his rival, Charles of Blois, went to welcome him. His cowardly attempt against the Constable Clisson again compromised his reputation, and was disgracefully avenged upon his son by the implacable daughter of Clisson.

The old ducal castle still rises on the left bank of the river. It was here Anne of Brittany was born, and here she married, 1499, her old admirer, the chivalrous Duke of Orleans, then King Louis XII., according to her stipulation, that the King, "viendra l'espouser en sa maison de Nantes." Left at the age of eleven, by the death of her father, a prey to claimants to her hand, which carried with it the powerful duchy of Brittany, Anne was a prize worth a king's seeking, even at a time when there were so many other rich heiresses undisposed of—Mary of Burgundy, Elizabeth of York, Isabella of Castille, and Catherine de Foix. Anne is described as handsome, but slightly lame, generous, and gentle, but grave and proud in her demeanour. Louis XII. called her his "fière Bretonne," and allowed her the uncontrolled government of Brittany, "tout ainsi que si elle n'estoit point sa femme."

Though the wife of two Kings of France, Anne never forgot the interests of her duchy, whose nationality she always strove to maintain with the pertinacity of a true Breton, and showed herself, by her spirit and independence, to be the most worthy of all her race to wear the ducal crown. Jean Marot addresses her as "Royne incomparable, deux fois devinement sacrée, Anne Duchesse de Bretagne."

Like most of the ladies of her age, Anne was an accomplished linguist. She understood Latin and Greek, and most of the European languages. She corresponded with her husband in Latin verse. Her letters, still extant, breathe the most tender affection. One, written to him (1499) during the Italian wars, begins, "Une épouse tendre et chérie écrit à son époux encore plus chéri, l'objet à la fois de ses regrets et de son estime, conduit par la gloire loin de sa patrie. Amante infortunée, il n'est pour elle aucun instant sans alarmes. Quel malheur affreux que celui d'être privé d'un Prince que l'on aime, d'un Prince plus amant qu'époux."

It was in this castle that Henry IV. signed his celebrated Edict of Nantes, so fatally revoked by Louis XIV.

The Duc de Mercœur, when governor of Brittany, made Nantes a regular fortified town. Having married Marie de Luxembourg, heiress of the house of Penthièvre, he sought to secure to himself the duchy of Brittany, while his brother, the Duke de Guise, aimed at the crown of France. Head of the League in that province, he looked upon it as a means of attaining his end: his wife joined him in his plans of ambition, and they by turns tyrannized and caressed the Nantais, amusing them with fêtes, in which the Duchess condescended to dance with the townsfolk. For twenty years Mercœur held the province; but a peace was eventually signed between him and Henry IV., through the mediation of Gabrielle d'Estrées, whose son César de Vendôme, then four years of age, was affianced to the Duke de Mercœur's daughter, then only six. When Henry IV. made his entry into Nantes after the pacification, he observed, on surveying the fortifications, "Ventre Saint Gris, les Ducs de Bretagne n'étaient pas de petits compagnons."

Nantes has been the scene of many an act of vengeance on the part of the Kings of France.

The Place du Bouffay, the place of execution, was the scene of the tragic death of the young Henri de Talleyrand, Comte de Chalais, executed by Louis XIII. for his part in the conspiracy which bears his name. Its object was the death of the Cardinal, and to place the crown on the head of the feeble Gaston, who was celebrating his marriage at Nantes at the time that his victim Chalais was paying the penalty of his crime.

The restless, intriguing Cardinal de Retz was imprisoned in Nantes Castle during the minority of Louis XIV., and made a wonderful escape by letting himself down from the walls to the river, where a boat awaited him. It was also at Nantes that the same monarch caused Fouquet to be arrested, not, as alleged, for his malpractices in office, but because his ambition and pomp offended the pride of his royal master.

For their part in the conspiracy of Cellamare, the Marquis de Poncallec and three other Breton gentlemen suffered on the Place du Bouffay, and the Vendean chief, La Charette, was also there shot in 1795.

Not far from the castle is the Rue Haute du Château. At the Maison Juigny, in this street, the Duchesse de Berri was arrested, after having remained sixteen hours concealed in an aperture behind a chimney on the third floor, scarcely a foot and a half high and four feet long. The police, having information of her being in the house, through the treachery of a Jew, had made a fruitless search, but had left a watch behind. The soldiers lighted a fire in the chimney, and the Duchess, with her three attendants, sallied out, her dress completely scorched. They had endured the heat, but were unable to bear the suffocation.

Nantes has some fine promenades and boulevards, planted with trees. In the Cours Saint Pierre and St. André are statues of the Duchess Anne and of the three Breton constables, Du Guesclin, Clisson, and Richmont.

One of the leading characteristics of Nantes is its numerous bridges: a regular chain of them form a continuous line across the river and canals, and others unite the islands which form the suburbs to the town itself.

The Museum contains a large collection of pictures, which the bequest of the Duke de Feltre (Maréchal Clarke) has increased considerably. These consist mostly of sketches by Paul Delaroche, and the charming Italian subjects of Léopold Robert.

"L'enfant charitable"—a nun on her deathbed embracing a child who is standing by her side, an angel behind—is a touching composition of Ary

Schäeffer. Another, by Paul Baudry, represents the death of Marat: Charlotte Corday's open, handsome face, looks incapable of the crime she has just perpetrated. There is one by Ziegler—Daniel in the lion's den—an angel staying the lions from molesting him. The atmosphere of light surrounding the angel is wonderful and unearthly. These two are in the general collection, together with numerous examples of the old masters.

Near our hotel is one of the curiosities of Nantes, the Passage de la Pommeraye, consisting of three stories of iron galleries or arcades, uniting the Rue de Crébillon with the Rue de la Fosse. The second arcade communicates by a flight of stairs with the third, called the Galerie de la Fosse, opening upon the street of that name.

The Garden of Plants is beautifully laid out; groves and avenues of magnolias in full flower, with rocks, waterfalls, rustic bridges, all most picturesquely disposed, making it one of the prettiest gardens and public promenades in France.

We descended the Loire by steamer, passing by vast granite buildings, built as magazines for colonial imports, called Les Salorges, in front of which the horrible noyades of Carrier took place, and these warehouses served as a temporary place of confinement for the victims. We next steamed past the island of Indret, the great manufacture of steam-engines for the State. Here we landed some market women, in caps of the same form, with high combs, as those of clear muslin worn by the Nantaises, only of a coarse material, and edged with black. On the right was Couëron, where Duke Francis II. died in consequence of a fall from his horse. The battle of St. Aubin-du-Cormier had decided his fate and that of his daughters,— a humiliation from which he never recovered. His faithful friend Rieux, who commanded his army, defeated by the youthful Louis de la Trémouille; the chivalrous Louis of Orleans, a prisoner in an iron cage in the " Grosse Tour" at Bourges; and the safety of his daughters at the mercy of King Charles VIII., or worse, of his imperious sister, the Regent Anne de Beaujeu, who would have committed some act of spoliation, had not the Chancellor Rochefort saved the duchy by his integrity, declaring to Anne that " a conqueror without right is but an illustrious robber."

At Les Pellerins, barges were loading with hay, and heaps of it standing on the river's edge ready for embarkation. On the left bank is Paimbœuf, where diligences run to Pornic, a favourite little watering-place south of the Loire.

St. Nazaire is a bustling seaport town, now the point of departure of the transatlantic steamers for the West Indies and Mexico. A Mexican, in his picturesque costume, all the seams of his dress fringed with hanging silver buttons, was living in the same hotel with ourselves. St. Nazaire has now a large floating basin, opened in 1858, capable of holding 200 ships of large size, and another is in course of construction.

It was from St. Nazaire that Prince Charles, the young Pretender, sailed on the adventurous expedition of '45, furnished with a frigate and a ship of the line by Mr. Walsh, of Nantes. Among the noble cavaliers who had sacrificed everything to follow the Stuarts into exile was the Walsh family, originally from Ireland. They had shared the wandering fortunes of Charles II., returned with him at the Restoration to find the greater part of their property confiscated; but they did not hesitate to sacrifice the rest when James II. abdicated the throne, and a Walsh commanded the ship which carried the King to France. Sent on a secret mission to England, he was recognized, denounced, and arrested. James II. created him an Earl at St. Germain. Two of his sons had retired to St. Malo and Nantes, and engaged in commercial speculations, endeavouring thereby to restore the fortunes of their house. Commerce was strictly forbidden to the Breton nobles; but, when war or misfortune had reduced their fortunes, they were allowed to enter into commerce, or any other profession, without derogating from their rank, provided they first deposited their swords with the Parliament, to be again claimed when their circumstances were improved. All will remember the anecdote in the 'Sentimental Journey.' As a book, called 'The State of Nobility in Brittany,' published in 1681, sets forth: "When nobles are engaged in commerce, their noble blood sleeps; but when the derogatory works are over, it revives. It is never lost but in death." But to return to the Walsh family. One of the brothers had embarked the remains of his little fortune in the business of "armateur"—a kind of shipowner, or one who fits out and charters ships, and sometimes commands them himself—the profession of Jean Bart and Duguay Trouin.[1] It was to this Anthony Walsh, and a banker of Dunkirk, that Prince Charles addressed himself to fit out an old worm-eaten seventy-gun man-of-war, the 'Elizabeth,' they had just obtained from Government for his expedition. True to the hereditary loyalty of his family, Mr. Walsh not only devoted all he possessed to the armament of the frigate, but also fitted out a brig, called the 'Doutelle'—both intended as privateers to cruise against the English—and took the command of her himself. On the

---

[1] The late Vicomte Walsh has written 'Gilles de Bretagne,' and other novels, with all a Breton's nationality. His son, the present representative of the family, occupies the beautiful Château of Chaumont on the Loire, devolved to him by right of his accomplished wife, the widow of the Comte d'Aramon.

28th June, 1745, furnished with about 4000*l.* of money, Charles Edward embarked on the Loire, in a fisherman's boat, to join the 'Doutelle' at St. Nazaire, and the 'Elizabeth' at Belle-Isle. He passed for a young Irish priest, and wore the habit of a student of the Scots' College at Paris. The ships encountered an English man-of-war, the 'Lion.' At the sound of the first shot, the Prince rushed on deck and asked for a sword. Mr. Walsh, by virtue of his authority as captain, took him by the arm and said to him sternly, "M. Abbé, your place is not here; go below with the passengers." The Prince obeyed, night separated the combatants, and on the 18th of July he was safely landed in Scotland. On Michaelmas Day, the following year, the disasters of Culloden again threw him an exile on the shores of Brittany.

From St. Nazaire we took a carriage for Guérande, to visit that remarkable district called the Canton de Croisic, and consisting chiefly of that place and the Bourg de Batz. We first came to Escoublac, a corruption of Episcopi lacus, deriving its name from a lake belonging to the bishop of the diocese.

The old town has been entirely buried by the moving sands which have blown over it, and, in 1779, its inhabitants transferred their houses to the present site. Hills of sand surround it in every direction.

Here we left the high road, and turned off to the left to Poulignan, a little white bay, as its name implies; a charming retreat, with beautiful white sands and picturesque rocks. This is a favourite watering-place with the Nantais. Its whole population appeared to be in the water. A row of small wooden châlets are built along the shore for the bathers, no machines are used.

From Escoublac begins the large extent of salt-pans in which consist the riches of this country. They reach to Batz and Le Croisic, the peninsula which forms this district having formerly been an island which gradually has been transformed into a marsh.

These salt-pans, cut out into small squares, have the appearance of one great chess-board, interspersed with occasional hamlets and woods. The working of them employs the whole population of the district.

They consist of large basins, dug at different depths, into which the water of the sea is introduced, and are divided into squares called "œillets." The salt-water is turned upon the marsh by canals styled "étiers," edged with narrow paths or roads called "bossis," elevated, some of them, three or four feet above the marsh; on these the newly collected salt is generally laid. The water passes by a subterranean conduit, the "coëf," into the "vasière," where the first evaporation takes place; and then successively into the "cobiers," "fares," and "adernemètres," until it flows finally into the "œillets," where the salt is definitively formed. Each "œillet" is about 20 feet by 30. The heat of the sun and the wind effect the evaporation, which the paludier assists by stirring the water from time to time. The salt which forms on the surface resembles a kind of white cream, and exhales an agreeable perfume resembling violets. This is the finest salt; that which falls to the bottom of the salt-pan is of a greyish cast. The salt when formed is then scraped off, drained, and the women collect it and stack it on the "bossis" into conical heaps, which they cover with a coating of clay, to render them impervious to weather. In the salting season, the salt marshes with their innumerable hillocks of white salt have the appearance of a vast tent-covered camp. Each "œillet" produces about 150 lbs. of salt. The same salt-pans are worked from century to century by the same "paludiers" or their descendants. The proprietors may change, but the workmen remain, considering the salt-pans their prescriptive inheritance. For payment, they receive one-fourth of the salt. The dress of the paludier is a smock-frock of irreproachable whiteness, with pockets, white shoes, gaiters, and linen breeches, an enormous black flap hat turned up on the side in a point or horn. The

Salt-pans, with Le Croisic in the distance.

young man wears the point over the ear, the married turns it behind, and the widower in front. We reached the Bourg de Batz in time for vespers, and had an opportunity of seeing the people in their

45. Paludier of the Bourg de Batz, in his working dress.

Sunday dress. The men wear three or four cloth waistcoats, all of different lengths, so as to let the various colours, red, white, and blue, with which they are bound, appear one above the other in tiers, a muslin turnover collar, full plaited breeches of fine cloth tied at the knee by garters of floating ribbon, white woollen stockings with worked clocks and light yellow shoes, their flap hats ornamented with a roll of chenille of varied colours. The head-dress of the women is singular and most intricate. The hair, in two rolls, twisted round with white tape, forms a kind of coronet across their heads; over this, a piece of net is drawn tight, forming a sort of cap, describing a peak behind, and crossing in front like a handkerchief.

The dress consists of several petticoats of cloth plaited, red body, turned-up sleeves, and large coloured bibs or plastrons which they call "pièces," of the same stuff as their dresses. The girls' aprons are plain, without pockets, but the women's are of coloured silk, some of a rich brocade. A shawl with fringed border completes the costume. Some of the women had their heads and shoulders wrapped up in a triangular, black, shaggy sheepskin mantle; these were widows.

At the inn where we alighted, they keep the splendid costumes worn by the people at weddings and other great occasions; and, by paying them for their trouble, they will put them on for inspection. The bride's costumes are of great magnificence; they array themselves in three different dresses on their wedding-day. First, a gown of white velvet, with apron of moire antique; secondly, one of violet velvet; and the third equally costly. Embroidered sleeves, the "pièce" of cloth of gold, the petticoats looped up with a wide sash, embroidered in gold, and gold clocks to the stockings.

46. Paludier of the Bourg de Batz, in his wedding dress.

We were shown a state bed, or "lit de mariage," a tall four-post, painted red, with green reps tester and curtains, embroidered with yellow chenille. The great sign of wealth is to have the bedding reach to the top of the bedstead. To effect this, the base is formed of bundles of vine-stalks, over which is spread the straw, and when this scaffolding has been raised some feet, a paillasse is placed over it, then the feather-bed, so that it literally requires a ladder to ascend to the top of this mountain of bedding, and then it is difficult to crawl into it. There were a bolster and two pillows covered with velvet, which, with the sheets, were all trimmed with a kind of lace or cutwork.

The houses are solidly built of granite, and slated; the windows large. The furniture is good, generally comprising a well-waxed carved oak armoire, upon which are arranged earthenware plates of various colours.

The paludiers of Batz preserve their original type distinct from the peasants of the environs; and form, like the Jews, a separate people, intermarrying among themselves, retaining their own peculiar manners and customs. They are supposed to descend from a Saxon colony. The paludier is tall in stature; their women remarkable for their fair complexions, which contrast strongly with their sunburnt neighbours. They are loyal and devout, true to their word, courageous and enduring; though the paludier is miserably poor, from the oppressiveness of the salt-tax, he never complains. Begging is unknown. Their food consists of rye bread, porridge of black corn, potatoes, and shellfish. They are sober, and drink wine in small quantities.

Formerly the salt was distributed over the adjacent provinces by means of "saulniers," the journeymen labourers of the paludiers. Dressed in their picturesque costume, with a train of mules, whose tinkling bells announced their arrival, the saulnier was welcomed in every village where he sold his salt or exchanged it for other merchandize. "Le sucre des pauvres," as salt has been aptly called, was severely taxed under the old régime; distributions of the "sel royale" were yearly made by the Government among the gentry of the provinces, but the poor, who had no such privileges, severely felt the oppression, and smuggling was consequently extensively carried on, and the "faux saulnier," with his double bag across his shoulders, secretly sold salt upon which the gabelle had not been paid. With a faux saulnier originated the great peasant rising in Brittany, the Chouan war; a war to which Napoleon said, "All preceding wars have been but games." Jean, father of the four brothers Cottereau, was a maker of wooden shoes, and lived in a forest near Laval (Maine). From his solitary life he had acquired such sombre, wild, melancholy habits, that people gave him the name of Chouan, Maine patois for Chat-huant, and his family received the sobriquet long before the insurrection of 1792. Jean

Cottereau was the most celebrated faux saulnier of Maine; he had accidentally killed a revenue officer in one of his encounters, and his heroic mother made a journey to Versailles, barefooted, "sur le cuir de ses pieds," to obtain his pardon. Jean's master and patron was guillotined, his two sisters shared the same fate, and one of his brothers died of his wounds, and his body was disinterred by the Revolutionists. These personal wrongs, the treatment of the King, the interdiction of the Catholic religion, its processions, its bells, the persecution of its ministers, all goaded the Breton peasantry to revolt; and Jean was the first to fire a gun against a Republican at the cry of "Vive le Roi." The rising began with a few peasants, armed with a gun or a stick, dressed in short breeches open at the knee, with leather gaiters, and coloured garters; their long hair streaming over the shoulders, their heads covered with a wide-brimmed hat, or brown or red cap, sabots tipped with iron, and, in cold weather, a loose coat of goatskin. The Chouans assembled in small bands and attacked the Republicans at night in ambuscade, and when they had killed a few "Bleus" disappeared among the corn-fields or the furze-bushes. Simple peasants, they fought against the Republicans in defence of the altar and the throne. Their "commandements" ran thus:—

> "Ton Dieu, ton Roy, tu serviras
> Jusqu'à la mort fidèlement.
> Docile à tes chefs tu seras,
> Afin de vaincre surement.
> Sobre et discret te montreras,
> Buvant peu, parlant rarement ;
> De ton chef jamais n'agiras
> Attendant le commandement ;
> Violemment rien ne prendras,
> Mais en payant exactement.
> Age et sexe respecteras,
> Etant soldat et non brigand.
> Les comités corrigeras,
> Et les mouchards chrétiennement ;
> Né Breton, tu n'oublieras,
> Afin d'agir loyalement.
> Dans le succès clement seras ;
> Dans le malheur, ferme et constant.
> Chaque jour ton Dieu tu prieras ;
> Que peux tu sans son bras puissant?"

Such were the first Chouans: they had no organisation until they followed Larochejaquelin and the Vendean army to Granville, and accompanied them in their retreat; when their numbers were materially increased and their character completely changed by the deserters and brigands, who joined and eventually succeeded the peasantry.

The church of Batz is of cut stone. It has a square tower, surmounted by a cupola steeple, which with that of Le Croisic serves as a landmark to vessels having to steer between the two dangerous rocks Le Four, in front of Le Croisic, and Les Blanches, situated near the mouth of the Loire.

The choir is inclined, like that of St. Pol and others in Brittany. On one of the bosses in the interior is a grotesque carving of a man torn to pieces by the seven capital sins. On others are the Santa Veronica, the Good Shepherd, Ste. Barbara, &c. Near the church are the pretty ruins of the chapel of Notre Dame-du-Mûrier.

We drove on to Le Croisic, in Breton, "Little Cross;" so called from the small chapel of the Crucifix, built to commemorate the baptism by St. Felix, Bishop of Nantes, in the sixth century, of the Saxon colony who occupied the peninsula. Le Croisic was one of the first towns in Brittany which received Christianity, and bears for its arms a cross between four ermines. Along the road-side are cisterns or wells dug in the sand, and girls were filling with water the classical stone pitchers they carried upon their heads—quite an Eastern picture, suggestive of Rebecca and the damsels of her country. Le Croisic is almost surrounded by the sea, low, and without shelter, which renders it cold, damp, and exposed to the winds; turf is almost the only fuel used.

It is much frequented as a watering-place, and has an Etablissement. It is also a sea-port, with a rocky entrance to the harbour, and the dangerous rock with its lighthouse, called Le Four, extending for a league in front. The inhabitants of Le Croisic are principally engaged in the sardine fishery, and the curing of these fish consumes much of the salt of the marshes. The people complain this year they have no large orders for sardines, and there is but little white salt.

The chapel of St. Goustan, on the edge of the harbour, is singularly built; its western gable perched upon a little rock, half of which is inside and half outside the building. The church is no longer open for Divine service; but the peasant-girl who desires to know if she will be married this year, tries to pass a pin through the bars of the northern window without touching the wall. On the opposite side of the estuary are Périac and La Turbale, both seats of the sardine fishery. Returning the way we came, we stopped at the Plage Valentin, another bathing-place in a pretty little bay; with dressing-rooms and a small Etablissement. An omnibus conveys the bathers from Le Croisic, for two sous. The sea looks more inviting here and at Poulignan than at Le Croisic, where there is so much sea-weed in the harbour. We returned through Batz; the cathedral tower of Saint Aubin at Guérande is to be seen at a great distance, and is a prominent object in the scenery; the whole country is covered with salt-pans. Guérande stands on a height, and turning back, the view of the whole district is most extensive. We passed through Saillé, where

Duke John IV. married Joan of Navarre, afterwards the second wife of Henry of Lancaster.

Guérande, built on a vine-covered granite slope, is a singular old feudal town of the fifteenth century. It was fortified by Duke John V., and is nearly surrounded by granite walls, with ten towers and four old gateways, placed at the cardinal points of the compass. St. Michel, the principal gate, or rather a fortress, is flanked by two high towers, and contains the prison, archives, and hôtel de ville. A moat formerly surrounded the walls; but it has long been filled in, and boulevards substituted. From the battlements hang festoons of honeysuckle and ivy, and the moat is full of the yellow iris and water-lilies; nevertheless, Guérande has an austere, sombre aspect. There is a fine terrace walk, called the Mail, commanding a view of the whole country over Poulignan, Batz, and Le Croisic—a tented plain of salt.

The church of St. Aubin has Romanesque columns, with grotesque capitals. In one, two persons are sawing a third, stretched upon a wheel. On the left of the double-arched porch, is a pulpit outside the church, and there is some good painted glass within. Notre Dame Blanche, a chapel of the fourteenth century, is a pretty little building with stone pulpit and a sculptured group of Notre Dame-de-la-Salette with the two peasant children of Alsace.

Next day, we took a private carriage for La Roche Bernard; the road lying over a wide extent of land through Herbignac to La Roche Bernard (Morbihan), which is most picturesquely situated on a rocky height overhanging the Vilaine, here tra-

47.   La Roche Bernard.

versed by an elegant suspension-bridge, opened in 1839, about 666 feet long and above 108 feet above high-water mark—a terrible dizzy height to cross even in calm weather. A few years since, the postman, his cart, and horse were all blown over into the river, and nothing more was ever heard of them.

We went fishing several days in a large étang close to La Roche Bernard, and one evening took a pretty walk over the hills to another pond situated in a lovely secluded valley near a water-mill. La Roche Bernard was an early Protestant colony, founded by the Sieur d'Andelot, Seigneur of La Roche Bernard, brother to Admiral Coligny, and one of the firmest supporters of Calvinism. The Calvinists used to assemble at his château of Bretesch, where the minister of La Roche Bernard came to preach to them. D'Andelot and his sister, who was equally zealous in the cause, are, it is said, interred at La Roche Bernard. Near the Halles is a square block of houses; one of timber, with "Voie au Duc" inscribed upon it. These houses are said to have belonged to a Protestant community, and all to communicate with each other.

The evening of our arrival there was a wedding supper given at our hotel, the grand dinner having taken place elsewhere. The bride wore a white sash, with wreaths of white flowers round her Nantais cap. After supper the party danced Breton "ronds." The dancers form a large ring (grand rond), holding each other's hands, which they swing violently as they sidle round in a kind of hop-skip-and-a-jump step, accompanied by singing in a most monotonous tone. This went on until midnight. This kind of dance dates, they say, from Celtic times. The music consists of the biniou or bagpipe, and the flageolet or hautboy, sometimes with the addition of a drum. The biniou, cornemuse, or bagpipe, is the national instrument of western and southern France. How it came to be introduced into Scotland and expel the harp—which was as much the original music of Scotland as of Wales and Ireland—is a mystery. But, as in the sixteenth century the harp went out and the bagpipes came into fashion, it may be surmised that it was brought in, with other French novelties, on the return of Queen Mary, perhaps by the Queen herself, or, maybe, some itinerant player of the cornemuse may have accidentally been in her train, and his music set a fashion which has now become national.

On market-day numbers of the women from Muzillac, a place about ten miles distant, came in with their fruit. They all wear an enormous plaited black cap, which looks like the cowl of a friar. The graceful form of the earthenware pots attracted our attention: probably they came from the adjacent town of Herbignac. The 15th August, Fête de la Vierge, and also that of the Emperor, was kept as a general holiday. An immense concourse of people arrived from the neighbourhood, and attended the six o'clock mass. We walked to the quay, to see the sports on the water; the spectators picturesquely grouped on a mass of bare rocks, commanding a pretty view up and down the river.

The amusements consisted of some races, and a mât de cocagne, or greased pole, placed horizontally over the river; the feat being to walk safely to the end, where the prize was fixed, without falling into the water. In the evening "ronds" were danced, and every house had illuminations, in the shape of a candle stuck in a potato, and placed on each end of the window sill.

Next day we left by diligence for Vannes, passing through Muzillac and on to Auray, where we took the steamer for Belle Isle.

A steamer sails daily from the quay at Auray. The banks of the River Loch are very picturesque, the pine-trees (*Pinus maritima*) growing to the water's edge. On the left, the islands of the Morbihan; on the right, Locmariaker; the view extending to Carnac and Mont St. Michel, over the whole sweep of the bay formed by the peninsula of Quiberon.

At Port Navalo we emerged from the Morbihan, and, on our right, passed the little rocky island of Teigneuse, with its lighthouse; and, on the left, those of Houat and Haedik (the duck and the duckling); the former famous as the retreat of St. Gildas, who leaped from here with one bound, a distance of ten miles, to the peninsula of Rhuys, where he built his monastery. From Auray to Belle Isle is in all forty-eight miles—ten miles of river to Port

Navalo, the rest open sea. After eight hours' sail we reached Le Palais, the port and principal town of Belle Isle, built on the north-east side, and overhung by the citadel, the work of Vauban. The town consists of one principal street—the Rue Trochu—so called after the General of that name and his brother, who were the first, at the beginning of this century, to introduce agriculture into the island. We passed, at a distance to the right, the model farm of M. Trochu fils, on our way across the island to the lighthouse,—a cheerless drive, as there are no trees to be seen except near Le Palais. When M. Trochu commenced his labours, agriculture was little attended to in France, but he persevered in his exertions, beginning by clearing about sixty acres of granite rock, a land covered with heath and furze, setting at defiance the Breton saying, "Lande tu fus, lande tu es, lande tu seras." This same district is now covered with rich meadows, fine woods, productive arable fields, and magnificent pasture land, on which horses are extensively reared.

We gathered on the heathy moor three kinds of heath, the Cornish among others. The artichoke grows wild in the waste grounds. Wheat, turnips, beetroot, Indian corn, and potatoes, are the chief produce of the land in cultivation. This last vegetable was introduced by the families from Nova

Scotia (Acadia), who settled in Belle Isle, after that province was ceded to England by the Treaty of Paris, in 1766. This was several years before Parmentier had extended the use of the potato, or "truffe rouge," as it was first called, over other parts of France. Indian corn was probably also brought in by the Nova Scotians. The leaves are constantly cut during its growth as fodder for the cattle, so that the cob hardly attains a foot in height from the ground. On the left of our road we saw in the distance the village of Bangor, which gives its name to one of the four districts into which Belle Isle is divided. A little south is the fine granite lighthouse, of the stupendous height of 450 feet. We toiled up 255 steps (223 stone and 32 iron) before we gained the lantern, and, though the view was very extensive, we were rejoieed at finding ourselves safe down. One of the guardians had been waylaid, kicked, and beaten, a few evenings before, for some slight grudge. He seemed in great suffering, but had no doctor; the Breton, in his simple confiding faith—that with the Almighty are the issues of life and death, and that illness will end according to His decree—considers the calling in of a medical adviser but an unnecessary expense to his family. From the lighthouse we walked to the sea-shore. Belle Isle is a table-land, surrounded by steep cliffs, averaging 130 feet in height, which can only be

Entrance to Le Palais, Belle Isle.

descended to the shore in particular places. We walked to the Grotte du Port Coton, where begins the "Mer Sauvage," as it is called, an extent of five to six miles of most picturesque rocks, some elevated from 130 to 160 feet above the level of the sea, jagged and torn into most fantastic forms by the ceaseless dashing of the waters of the Atlantic, which have formed various grottoes in the cliffs. We descended into one of these caverns by a narrow gulley, but could not proceed far, as the tide was entering fast, and would soon have surrounded us, cutting off all means of retreat.

It reminded us of the description in the 'Vicomte de Bragelonne' of the grotto at Locmaria, which was blown up, and crushed the mousquetaire Porthos, at the moment of his and Aramis' triumph over the soldiers of the King. So great at times is the fury of the waves, that our guide at the lighthouse told us he had seen on several occasions the spray driven over to Le Palais, nearly five miles distant. Continuing our walk along the cliffs, we came to an enormous mass of rock, standing far out detached from the cliff, and covered with screaming sea-gulls. We again descended by another fissure into a pretty sandy cove, surrounded by the same wild granite rocks; but in most places there is no beach at all. It was now high water, so it was useless to attempt the Grotte des Apothécaires,—the finest, they say, of them all, and we returned to Le Palais well pleased with the remarkably wild coast we had seen. Belle-isle forms now a canton in the department of Morbihan. In ancient days it belonged to the Abbot of Saint-Croix, at Quimperlé, who sold it, in the time of Charles IX., to the Maréchal de Gondi, and, in 1573, it was erected into a Marquisate. (Cardinal de Retz lived here after his escape from the castle of Nantes.) One of his successors, Henri de Gondi, being overwhelmed with debt, sold the island to Nicolas Fouquet, the ill-fated Superintendent of Finance, on whose disgrace, and his being subsequently consigned to the fortress of Pignarol, his grandson, the Marquis de Belle Isle, exchanged it with Louis XV. for the Comté of Gisors, erected into a duchy in 1742. Fouquet built a palace and completed the citadel, for which he employed Vauban. He also projected fortifications to enclose the town, which are now in course of completion by the Emperor, after Vauban's plans. Several guns had just been landed, the day before we visited the citadel, to see which an order is requisite. Near the citadel is the "Maison centrale des détenus," now only containing a few old men, too feeble for hard labour. We were too tired to walk to look at the celebrated cistern of Vauban, which holds, we were told, above thirty thousand imperial gallons of water. Fouquet's palace was, it is said, destroyed to complete the line of fortifications. A house was pointed out to us as having formed part of the original building. Some years since, a stone was picked up in the harbour bearing his ambitious device—a squirrel, with the motto, *Quo non ascendum?* "To where shall I not rise?" The greater number of the population of Belle Isle are employed in the fisheries; of these the sardine and the tunny are the chief. There are large establishments for curing sardines, which are very abundant, and lobsters, taken in the rocks of Belle Isle and the little islands of Houat and Hædic, are sent to London and Paris. The boats go as far as Spain, to the coast of Catalonia, for the tunny fishery, which extends from August to the beginning of October. These fish are taken by lines hung along the sides of the vessel, with a bell attached to each to give notice of a bite. The most esteemed part of the tunny is the underneath, or "panse." The next morning we sailed back to Auray. The nearest point to Belle Isle is Quiberon, only ten miles from Le Palais. From Auray by rail to Quimper, where we took the diligence to Pont l'Abbé, an old town formerly of

49.   Device of Fouquet.

some importance, in the midst of a fertile, rich country. The costume worn at Pont l'Abbé and along the Bay of Audierne is very singular. The cap, or "bigouden," is composed of two pieces: first, a kind

50.   Peasant Girl.   Pont l'Abbé.

of skull-cap, or serre-tête, fitting tight to the head over the ears, then a little round bit, resembling, the young people said, a "pork-pie" hat, made of starched linen, pinched into a three-cornered peak, the middle peak embroidered and tied on by a piece of tape fastening under the chin; the hair is turned up, "en chignon," over the skull-cap. The body of the dress has a large "pièce" of red or yellow, and sleeves to match. The men wear several very short coats, one over the other, the shortest trimmed with fringe; sometimes sentences are embroidered with coloured woollens round the edge. It was market day; the women were sitting, with distaff and spindle, on each side of the entrance to the Halle. Some of them have short bead-chains with a ring, attached to the left shoulder, to stick their distaffs in when not at work. There was abundance of fruit and vegetables, potatoes, and sardines, which, with bigoudens and other articles of dress, formed the principal commodities for sale. Pont l'Abbé and its Port, Loctudy, carry on an extensive trade with Jersey, and large quantities of potatoes are exported to that island. There were some Jersey merchants at the table-d'hôte.

The church of Pont l'Abbé has only one aisle. There is a fine rose window over the west entrance, of great lightness and richness, with a smaller one at the left; at the east end is another rose window of larger dimensions, the mullions forming geometric patterns, but differing in design from the other. The French architects always took great pains in the decoration of this part of the church, and these wheel windows really rival those of Rouen.

Attached to the church, are the cloisters of the Carmelite convent to which the church formerly belonged, built in the beginning of the fifteenth

51.   Apse of the Church, Loctudy.

century by Bertram de Rosmadec, who had so much contributed to the completion of the cathedral at Quimper. The square is surrounded by an interlaced circular arcade, forming trefoiled pointed arches, all in excellent preservation. The access to the cloisters is through the conventual building, now a private house and garden, the proprietor kindly granting us permission.

We drove to Loctudy, on the mouth of the Pont l'Abbé river opposite the little island of Tudy, called after an English saint of that name. Fleeing from the persecutions of the Picts and Scots who desolated his country, he founded here, at the end of the fifth century, a considerable monastery, afterwards destroyed by the Normans.

At Loctudy is a curious Romanesque church, one of the best preserved in Brittany, which dates from the Templars of the twelfth century. It has a nave with aisles going all round the choir, and three round apsidal chapels at the end. The five arches on each side of the nave are horse-shoe shaped, and the choir is surrounded by the same number of high narrow arches, resting on columns with grotesque capitals of complicated design. The three chapels behind are seen through the opening; on one of the capitals is sculptured the cross of the Templars. The whole building is spoiled by whitewash.

> "Chevaliers en ce monde cy
> Ne peuvent vivre sans souci;
> Ils doivent le peuple defendre,
> Et leur sang pour la foi espandre."
>
> EUSTACHE DESCHAMPS.

We engaged a rough kind of vehicle, much like a butcher's cart, to visit the Torche de Penmarch, a rocky promonotory, so called from its fancied resemblance to a horse's head, forming the southern

52.   Torche of Penmarch.

extremity of the department of Finistère. The Torche is a mass of rocks separated from the mainland by a chasm called the "Saut de Moine," because an Irish saint, named Viaud, jumped across it on his landing. In rough weather, the noise made by the sea dashing against its sides and rushing through the crevices of the rocks, is said to be heard at Quimper, a distance of twenty-one miles. A line of rocks runs all along the coast, marked by a lighthouse at Penmarch; we proceeded to another group of rocks near which M. de Châtellier, a proprietor and antiquary of this country, has built a house for painting and enjoying the scenery. One of our party clambered down to see the "Trou d'Enfer," a tremendously deep hole in the rocks, the bottom covered with a pink sort of sea-weed, and the water as clear as crystal. The whole country is a dreary sandy level, with salt-marshes, over which we passed to the ruined church of St. Fiacre, and close by is that of St. Guenolé, both situated near the sea. The countryman who showed us the church, knelt reverently down at the threshold and put up a short prayer before he entered the sacred building. The general devoutness and strong faith of the Bretons is most impressive and genuine, mixed, no doubt, with great superstition; but, as Wesley says, "Heaven makes allowance for invincible ignorance, and blesses the faith notwithstanding the superstition."

St. Guenolé consists of an unfinished square tower, with crocketed pinnacles and a porch of considerable size, under a large mullioned window of the fifteenth century. On each side of the porch are rude sculptures of ships and fishes, not uncommon in these parts, set there to show the church has been built with the thank-offerings of the fisher population of the district. In our tour we met with several churches with this sign, evidences of the piety of the fishermen; indeed, at Dunkirk, when the church was burned down in the sixteenth century by the French, it was entirely rebuilt by the contribution called "le filet saint," from an ancient custom among the fishermen of having one net so called, the produce of which was set apart for the church.

53. Ship Sculptured on the Walls. Church of St. Guenolé, Penmarch.

Towards the lighthouse are the ruins of the old town of Penmarch, much celebrated in the maritime history of the fourteenth to sixteenth centuries; its commerce extended even to Spain, and the riches of its inhabitants were so surpassingly great, that they drank out of silver cups, and the lords of a manor near the Torche furnished the silk required to line the road traversed by religious processions, their wealth being due to the "viande de carême," that is to say, to the cod fishery. But the discovery of Newfoundland deprived them of this lucrative monopoly, and the ravages of Fontenelle le Ligueur

Church of St. Guenolé, Penmarch.

completed their ruin. All now is a scene of desolation. Penmarch has been called the Palmyra of Brittany.

Guy Eder Fontenelle, the Leaguer, who spread terror and devastation throughout Brittany in the sixteenth century, was a member of the Beaumanoir family; the name he adopted was that of one of the family estates. He was born in the Château of Beaumanoir (near Evran), and his elder brother early foresaw his guilty career. He escaped from college and united himself with a set of young men as lawless as himself; they formed themselves into a band, which soon became the dread of all Brittany. They ravaged the whole of Tréguier and Cornouaille, surprised the châteaux of Coëtfrec and others, took the church of Carhaix, which they fortified, and the towns of Paimpol, Lannion, and Landerneau, which they pillaged, Penmarch and Pontcroix, whence they carried off an immense booty and 300 vessels, with which they scoured the seas; and lastly, Douarnenez and the Island of Tristan (in 1595), whence fruitless attempts were made to dislodge them. For three years Fontenelle made this island his head-quarters, issuing from his stronghold to devastate the country. He murdered above fifteen hundred peasants at Plougastel, sank an English ship, without allowing her crew a moment to save themselves, imprisoned and tortured at Douarnenez all who fell into his hands. His victims never survived his cruelties more than three or four days, when their bodies were cast out into the bay to the fishes. These were only a few of his atrocities. As he called himself one of the leaders of the League in Brittany, the Duke de Mercœur, its chief, indignant at the barbarities perpetrated in its name, caused Fontenelle to be imprisoned, but he was liberated on paying a ransom; and, fearing he would give Douarnenez over to the Spaniards, Fontenelle was included in the pacification of Mercœur with Henry IV. But four years later he was implicated in the conspiracy of Biron; on which occasion all his old crimes were raked up against him, and he was condemned to be dragged on a hurdle, and broken alive upon the wheel, which sentence was executed on the Place de Grève at Paris in 1602. In consideration of the illustrious house to whom he belonged, the king granted that in the act of condemnation he should not go by his own name. We next went to see the church of Saint Nonna in the town, the largest of the numerous churches in the parish of Penmarch. Ships are sculptured in front of the tower, as at St. Guenolé. On the left of the porch is a pretty window, the mullions formed by three fleur de lis. In the church is a curious old painting styled, "Procession du vœu de Louis XIII." Portraits of the King, the Dauphin (Louis XIV.),

Anne of Austria, and Cardinal Richelieu, are introduced, and a view of the church of St. Nonna is in the background.

On our way home we passed, on the left, at Kerscaven, two menhirs, one curiously furrowed and shaped like a half-opened fan.

We had a pretty drive from Pont l'Abbé, with occasional views of the Bay of Audierne, extending from Penmarch to the Pointe du Raz. Midway the horse, going down a steep hill, fell, and we all found ourselves upon the road, but happily unhurt. We met numbers of peasants returning from the fair at Pontcroix; and our driver, a butcher by trade, coolly stopped the vehicle, to discourse with them on the price of stock, and to handle the sheep they had bought. Our drive was enlivened with occasional peeps of the Bay of Audierne till we reached the little port of that name, the view of which is very pretty. Audierne is approached by a bridge across the river or estuary At its entrance is a lighthouse, and on the right a sandy bay, with bathing-machines in the season.

55. Fleur-de-Lisé Window, Church of St. Nonna, Penmarch.

The town consists of three streets of cut granite houses, with the name of the builder and the date of their construction inscribed over the door. Fishing is the occupation of the inhabitants, and the table-

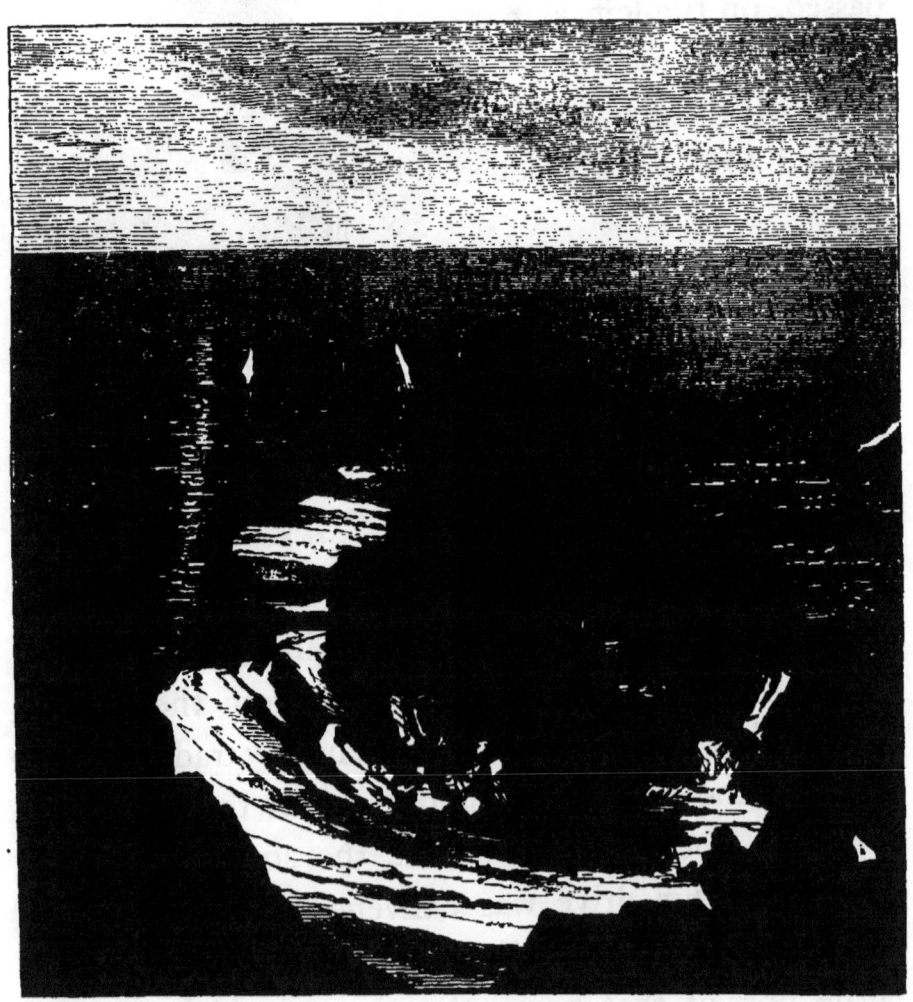

56. Pointe du Raz.

d'hôte at our comfortable, clean, little inn was plentifully supplied with magnificent john dorys, large red mullet, langoustes, and fish of every description.

From Audierne we took a carriage to visit the Pointe du Raz, a promonotory so famous for its rocks and wrecks. We went through a treeless country; near a pretty bay, on the left, is the chapel of Notre Dame-de-Bon-Voyage, destined chiefly for sailors, after which the country becomes more wild, barren, and cheerless. We passed over a bridge which no Breton would dare to cross at night, for fear of being flung by the spirits into the river. According to their belief, a hare appears on the bridge, and terrifies the horses, who throw their rider, and the traveller is dragged by the phantom into the muddy river, where he is kept till morning's dawn, when he is allowed to pursue his way, exhausted with cold, and half dead with fright. They are very superstitious here, as in all Cornouaille. A writer says, "every nation of the earth has its superstitions and absurdities, but Brittany has those of all other nations united." An old woman in a village hard by, said our driver, has never been seen inside the walls of a church; the people say she has sold herself to the evil one, and no one dares go near or speak to her.

On the left is the pretty steeple of the church of Plogoff, situated on an eminence, and dedicated to Saint Collédoc, a Welsh bishop of the sixth century, contemporary of King Arthur, and associated with many of the doings of Queen Guinevre and the knights of the Round Table. Lescoff is the last village we passed through before—after driving over a barren plain—we arrived at the lighthouse, built thirty years back at the Pointe.

We walked thence to the Pointe, a gigantic and magnificent mass of rocks, eighty feet above the level of the sea. We met with a good-natured woman, who led the young people over the rocks to look down the " Enfer de Plogoff." They had a slippery scramble to reach the hole, a kind of tunnel through which the sea rushes with great violence, so much more terrible than that of Penmarch, that the noise has been compared to the distant roaring of some thousands of wild beasts issuing from the depths of a forest. In the mean time, we remained seated on the bank enjoying the view. On the south lay the Bay of Audierne, extending in the form of a crescent, the promontories of Penmarch and Raz forming the extreme points. The currents, and the numerous rocks of the bay, render it a dangerous coast, formerly peopled by barbarous wreckers, who despoiled the shipwrecked mariners as our Cornish men of old. Opposite the Raz, about seven miles distant, is the Island of Sein, and to the right, the Baie des Trépassés. The island of Sein was anciently the seat of an oracle, interpreted by nine Druidesses, who were versed in every art and science. Moreover, they appear to have been accomplished needlewomen; for a Breton chronicler, giving an account of the corronation of an early king (Erech) at Nantes, describes his mantle as embroidered by these priestesses with figures of Arithmetic, Astronomy, and Music. Their skill in divination caused them to be associated with the fairies; and Morgan—*i.e.* "born of the sea"—one of these priestesses, who lived in the first century of the Christian era, was famous among the British fairies.

> " Avec succès cultivait la magie,
> Morgan de plus, était assez jolie."

Chateaubriand celebrates Velleda, the last of the Druidesses of Sein, tall in stature, her eyes blue, with long fair floating hair, dressed in a short black tunic, without sleeves, bearing a golden sickle suspended from a brazen girdle, and crowned with a branch of oak. Here King Arthur was brought by Merlin to recover of his wounds. The inhabitants of the island were celebrated for their ferocity as wreckers.

The passage between the island and the point or Bec du Raz—"qu'aucun n'a passé sans mal ou sans crainte"—is very dangerous, owing to the number of rocks and the violence of the currents; hence the well-known prayer of the Breton sailor, " Mon Dieu, secourez-moi pour traverser le Raz, car mon navire est petit et la mer est grande." Having no wish to run the risk of being detained at the island by rough weather, we did not attempt the passage.

The Baie des Trépassés, over which we looked on the right, is so called from the Celtic legend that the Druids embarked in this bay after their death, to be buried in the island of Sein:—

> "Autrefois, un esprit venait, d'une voix forte ;
> Appeler chaque nuit un pêcheur sur sa porte ;
> Arrivé dans la baie, on trouvait un bateau
> Si lourd et si chargé de morts qu'il faisait eau,
> Et pourtant il fallait, malgré vent et marée,
> Les mener jusqu'à Sein, jusqu'à l'île sacrée."
>
> BRIZEUX.

The bay also derives its name from the numerous shipwrecks that have taken place on its rocks, and from the number of corpses that have been floated there by the currents from ships foundered in the gulf comprised between the entrance of Brest, the Ouëssant Islands, and Sein. The whole extent of the coast of Brittany is one long wall of rocks, placed as it were to protect it from the inroads of the sea and from foreign invasion. Heaped one over the other, they resemble the bastions of a citadel, the advanced rocks extending out to sea, jutting up in every direction in endless reefs. Or its line of coast may be compared to the jagged teeth of a comb, with a second line of defence in the rocks further out to sea.

On the desolate shore of the Baie des Trépassés is a piece of water, the étang de Laoual, site of the city of Is—submerged by Divine vengeance, according to popular tradition, in the fifth century—a place of great commerce, arts, riches, and also of luxury. Gradlon, or Grallo, the king, alone attempted to stem the torrent. Built in the vast basin which now forms the Bay of Douarnenez, it was protected from the ocean by a strong dyke, the sluices only admitting sufficient water to supply the town. King Gradlon kept the silver key (which opened, at the same time, the great sluice and the city gates) suspended round his neck. His palace was of marble, cedar, and gold; in the midst of a brilliant Court sat enthroned his daughter Dahut, a princess who "had made a crown of her vices, and had taken for her pages the seven capital sins." Taking advantage of the sleep of her father, Dahut one night stole the silver key, and instead of opening the city gate, by mistake unlocked the sluices. The King was awakened by St. Guenolé, who commanded him to flee, as the torrent was reaching the palace. He mounted his horse, taking his worthless daughter behind him. The torrent was gaining upon him fast, when a voice from behind called out, "Throw the demon thou carriest into the sea, if thou dost not desire to perish." Dahut felt her strength failing her; the hands that convulsively grasped her father's waist relaxed their hold; she rolled into the water, disappeared, and the torrent immediately stopped its course. The King reached Quimper safe and sound, and that town became afterwards the capital of Cornouaille.

So runs the legend. That a great city once existed in the Bay of Douarnenez admits of no doubt. Besides the religious chronicles of the country, which have preserved the memory of its existence, in the sixteenth century, remains of old edifices were standing at the entrance of the bay, old paved roads have been traced, and walls found under water near the Pointe du Raz.

The tradition of a town thus swallowed up is common among the Celtic race. In Wales, the site of the submerged city is in Cardigan Bay; in Ireland, in Lough Neagh:—

> " On Lough Neagh's banks, where the fisherman strays,
>   At the hour of eve's declining,
>   He sees the round towers of other days
>   Beneath the waters shining."—MOORE.

One of our party went out fishing to the Pointe, and returned well laden with his spoils.

The road from Audierne to Douarnenez passes by Pontcroix, a little town on the same river (Goazien) as Audierne, along which the road runs—a charming drive. It has a magnificent Romanesque church of the twelfth (probably of the fifteenth) century, with a remarkable porch, richly embroidered in quatrefoils and trefoils. A tower in the centre, with octagonal spire is second to none in Cornouaille, except that

57.   Front of the Church, Pontcroix.

of Quimper. The arches of the nave are horseshoe, the transepts very narrow. Under the altar of the Lady Chapel is a "Cène," half the size of nature, sculptured in ivory and marble, of marvellous workmanship.

Eleven miles from Douarnenez we stopped to see the pretty little chapel of Notre Dame-de-Comfort, in a hamlet of that name, with light open-work steeple. Attached to one of the arches, on the left of the choir, is a wooden wheel, hung round with bells, to which is attached a long string. It is erroneously called "the wheel of fortune;" but is, in fact, the old wheel of sacring bells in use before the single bell was adopted.

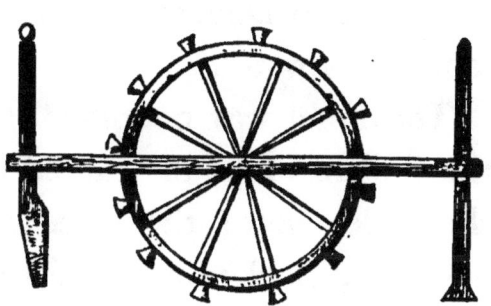

58. Wheel of Sacring Bells, Notre Dame de-Comfort, near Douarnenez.

The boy who showed us the chapel pulled the string which was fastened to a hook near the altar, and the wheel revolved and rang a merry peal. Formerly there was a little wooden figure attached to the wheel, which performed the same office. The road runs round a hill, along an estuary formed by the river, and suddenly the beautiful lake, called the Bay of Douarnenez, bursts on the sight, of a blue as lovely as the Italian seas.

The dirty little town of Douarnenez is charmingly

situated to the south of the bay, the hills clothed with trees to the water's edge. The Pointe du Raz forms the western boundary of the bay, and it is shut in to the north by the peninsula of Crozon; its extreme point, Pointe de la Chèvre, advancing nearly midway into the bay. The tide here falls eighteen feet. The triple peaks of the Méné-Hom, one of the Montagnes Noires, is a prominent feature in the view. Islands are scattered over the gulf, and the island of Tristan, retreat of Fontenelle le Ligueur, is so close to Douarnenez, that it may be reached on foot at low water.

The hotel was crammed, gentlemen sleeping on the billiard-table, or littered down in the room of the table-d'hôte: the place was crowded. All the world had flocked in to assist at the Pardon of Sainte Anne-la-Palue, which was to take place the following morning. No vehicle was to be had, and we were in despair of being able to go, when a good-natured voyageur kindly offered to drive us in his carriage—a proposal we thankfully accepted. In all our wanderings we had hitherto never been so fortunate as to see a Pardon, and we were very anxious to go.

The Pardon of Sainte Anne-la-Palue takes place the last Sunday in August, continuing three days, and is one of the most frequented in Finistère.

At Plonevez-Porzun we turned off the Crozon road, and about two miles further arrived at the chapel. The road all the way was lined with peasants walking to the Pardon. The young men of Douarnenez wear blue jackets, embroidered in colours, with rows of plated buttons, the sleeves and waistcoat

59. Costume of a Finistère Bride.

of a darker blue than the jacket, scarlet sashes, some with plaited bragou bras and shining leather gaiters; but most of them wore trowsers, their hair long, and their hats with two or three rows of coloured variegated chenille. The women had square caps, and aprons with bibs. Those who were in mourning wore light yellow caps, called "bourladins," stained that colour with beeswax or saffron.

St. Anne is a newly-built church, standing on the slope of a down which separates it from the sea, in a perfectly insulated situation. It is only opened once a year for the Pardon. Round it were erected numerous stalls, with toys, epinglettes, and rosaries (chapelets), in heaps for sale; for rosaries must always be purchased at the Pardon, to preserve the wearer from thunder and hydrophobia. The great fabric for them is at Angers, where they are made in immense quantities. In the principal manufactory a steam-engine is used for turning the beads; in the others the common lathe. One maker told us she sent annually into Brittany alone rosaries to the value of 800*l.* There were tents and booths erected for the accommodation of the pilgrims who had arrived the preceding day. They eat, drink, and dance in the tents by day, and sleep on the tables at night.

At ten o'clock, at the ringing of a bell, a procession was formed, consisting of a long line of peasants, preceded by priests and banners, which made the round of the church; the penitents, en chemise to the waist, barefooted, carrying wax-tapers in their hands. The penance is sometimes executed by proxy: a rich sinner may, for a small sum, get his penance performed by another. One woman made the round of the church on her knees, telling her beads as she hobbled along. This was in performance of a vow made for some special deliverance.

We proceeded to the top of the hill, from which the beautiful Bay of Douarnenez presented a most lively appearance; fleets of small boats arriving from every direction, and a huge steamer from Brest, which was obliged to land its passengers in small boats, on account of the shallowness of the water.

The appearance of the downs now became very animated, covered with gaily-dressed peasants arranged in groups, sitting or lying on the grass, in every kind of attitude.

At four o'clock the grand procession took place. First came the priests of all the surrounding districts, with the banners and crosses of their parishes; then followed five girls (three and two) in white, carrying a banner, and eight more in similar attire, bearing a statue of the Virgin. Next appeared the banner of Sainte Anne, carried by women in the gorgeous costume of the commune—gowns of cherry-coloured silk, trimmed half the way up with gold lace, a silver lace scarf, and aprons of gold tissue or rich silk brocade. Under their lace caps was a cap of gold or silver tissue. Four more of these superbly-dressed bearers ("porteuses") carried the statue of Ste. Anne.

Girls carrying blue flags walked by their side. Troops of barefooted penitents and shaggy-headed beggars

60.   Well of Ste. Anne-la-Palue.

closed the procession, which was followed by a countless train of the peasants. It slowly wound its way over the hill, and again descended to the church, where it mingled among the crowds of assembled spectators, which filled the churchyard and were seated on the steps of the calvary.

Not far from the church is the holy well of Ste. Anne, where devotees were engaged pouring the holy water over their hands and backs, dipping their children, and testing its miraculous efficacy by various other ablutions.

We proceeded next morning to Quimper, having had no opportunity of seeing Douarnenez itself. In the season it is a favourite watering-place, the bathing being about two miles from the town. It is a great place for the sardine fishery. From Quimper we went by rail to Rosporden, whence an omnibus runs to Concarneau. The church of Rosporden is situated on a little promontory, jutting out into a large étang fed by the river Aven, which runs through it and flows on to Pontaven.

We took a carriage at Rosporden for Le Faouët, passing by Scaër on the Isole, a stream which rises at the foot of the Montagnes Noires, takes a curve round the town of Scaër, and joins the Laita. It is full of trout and salmon.

Scaër is a town remarkable for having preserved many old customs and superstitions; among others, the bees are considered to be entitled to share in the joys and sorrows of the family. Their hives are surrounded with a red stuff on the occasion of a marriage; with a black on that of a death. This custom is still preserved in Wales. In all parts of Brittany bees are treated with special affection. As the redbreast is sacred, because she broke a thorn from the crown of our Lord that pierced His brow, so are the bees revered because, as we learn from the code of Hoel the Good, though they were sent from heaven to earth after the fall of man, the blessing of Heaven has ever followed them in their exile. This, too, is the reason the wax they produce has the privilege of lighting the altars for the divine office.

It was the day of a Pardon, and the peasants were all in gala dresses. A wrestling match unfortunately had just been finished; for throughout Cornouaille wrestling has been, from time immemorial, as favourite a game as in our county of the same name. Our driver tried without success to procure for us some of the little double crystals, intersecting each other at right angles, called "pierre de croix" —by mineralogists grenatite—found in the Coatdry, a small affluent of the Aven, washed out of the mica slaty rocks in which they abound. The peasants assign to them a miraculous origin, and wear them in little bags round the neck as charms against headache, blindness, shipwreck, and hydrophobia, being, as they

61. Cross Stones.

allege, signed with the cross. According to tradition, a pagan chief, having, in his impious rage, thrown down the cross in the chapel of Coatdry, Heaven, in memorial of the outrage, placed the sacred symbol upon the stones of the river.

At Le Faouët we again entered the department of the Morbihan. This pretty little town is situated between the Sterlaer and the Ellé. We first walked to see the chapel of Ste. Barbe, perched, in the most singular manner, in the cleft of a high rock, about a mile from the town.

After a steep climb we reached the plateau of the hill, where is the monument of a M. Berenger, who desired to be buried in this elevated spot, which commands a charming view of the surrounding country, the silvery waters of the Ellé winding at the base of the mountain. We then descended, by a flight of handsome, broad, granite steps, with balustrades, to the chapel, placed on so narrow a space that it was impossible to give it the usual inclination to the east. The entrance-porch is to the south-west, and the high altar opposite, against the walls of the chapel, to the north-east. On the top of the steps is the belfry, consisting of a roof, supported by four columns. The day of the Pardon each pilgrim rings the bell. The chapel was built in this singular spot, according to tradition, by a knight, who was overtaken by a storm in the valley of the Ellé beneath.

He saw an enormous mass of detached rock on the point of falling down and crushing him, when he invoked the intercession of Sainte Barbe, the guardian saint against thunder, promising to build her a chapel, if delivered from the danger. His prayer was heard; the rock was stayed in its descent and rested on the cleft, where, next day, the grateful knight began building the chapel, as a thank-offering for his escape. Above Ste. Barbe, stationed on an insulated rock, one of the highest peaks in Brittany, is a small chapel, dedicated to St. Michael, also approached by a flight of stone steps, like Ste. Barbe, with bridge built over an archway. The rock on which it stands is so abrupt, that rings are placed along the sides of the chapel for the pilgrims, when creeping round, to hold on by. Many have perished in the attempt; none, they say, have ever succeeded in making the circuit.

There was a wedding at Le Faouët during our stay there. Guests, invited from all quarters, to the number of 250, arrived in their gala costumes, some of them magnificent: one woman wore a gown entirely of gold tissue; it was her wedding-dress. The musicians, with biniou and hautboy, went round to summon the guests. We saw the procession going to church. The bride was prettily dressed, with a high cap, beautifully " got up," pointed in form, and trimmed with lace, and embroidered; a muslin apron, also lace-trimmed, and a double muslin shawl, similarly trimmed, the lace beautifully plaited; a violet silk dress, white moire sash, and a small bunch of white flowers. The bridegroom was "en bourgeois." Outside the church door were tables, laid out with cakes; after the service the bride and all the party took each a cake and put money in the plates, as an offering for the poor. They next adjourned to the Place, where they danced three "gavottes" under the trees. The ceremony of stealing away the bride then took place; that is, she was chased by some dozen of the youths of the company, and he who had the good fortune to capture her she treated to a cup of coffee at a café. Dinner followed, and then they returned to the interminable gavotte. They hold each other's hands "en grand rond," then wind themselves round the centre couple, executing most elaborate steps, and uncoil again to return to the grand rond. We counted as many as thirty couples in one gavotte. These festivities last two, or sometimes three, days, during which time all the wedding party are entertained free of expense.

Le Faouët is a great fishing quarter. The Ellé, which flows round the town, is a stream of considerable size; and, four miles below Le Faouët, it is joined by the Laita, and before Quimperlé unites its waters with the Isole, whence its mingled streams flow into the Atlantic, under the name of the Laita. We were told that large fish were taken in a pond in the grounds of the Abbey of Langonnet, not far from Le Faouët, but it is strictly preserved.

The people of this district retain all the old Breton superstitions; they believe in the Car of Death, drawn by six black horses, driven by the "Ankou," or Phantom of Death, with an iron whip. They also have full faith in the Washerwomen of the Night (Lavandières de la Nuit), who wash the shrouds for the dead, and fill the air with their melodious songs:—

> "Si chrétien ne vient nous sauver,
> Jusqu'au jugement faut laver:
> Au clair de la lune, au bruit du vent,
> Sous la neige, le linceul blanc."

> "If no good soul our hands will stay,
> We must toil on till judgment-day:
> In strong wind or clear moonlight,
> We must wash the death-shroud white."

They engage the passer-by to help them in wringing the linen; if he refuses, they drown him in their washing trough, or suffocate him in a wet sheet. Should he show himself ill-disposed, after having agreed to help them, they dislocate his arm. If he wrings the wrong way, his fate is inevitable; but if docile and obliging, they give him some clothes and dismiss him.

A mile and a half from Le Faouët, on a height a little off the Quimperlé road, is the beautiful

Rood-Screen or Jubé, St. Fiacre.

church of Saint Fiacre, dating from the middle of the fifteenth century, celebrated for its carved wooden jubé, or rood-screen, and its painted glass. The church is falling to decay. It would be tedious to enumerate all the figures, and describe the details of this beautiful jubé. The carving is a perfect tracery of lace-work. Three large figures represent our Saviour and the two thieves. Then there are the Virgin and St. Joseph; the latter, with carpenter's plane and hammer. Below, Adam and Eve, and the Angel with the flaming sword. Two angels hold cartouches, on one of which is inscribed, "L'an mil $_{\text{iiii}}^{\text{c}}$ $_{\text{iiii}}^{\text{xx}}$ (1480) fut fait cette sculpture par Olivier de Loergan;" and, on the other, "Cette passion fut peinte l'an 1627. Yves Perez fabricant. Tous repaint en 1866." Below are panels carved in the flamboyant style, of exquisite workmanship. The two middle panels have the sacred monogram, those on the east side ermines surrounded by cordelières.

The side of the rood-loft facing the choir has pendents with grotesque carvings of allegorical signification.

A man in an apple-tree, gathering the fruit, symbolizes theft. Next comes a disgusting representation of gluttony: a man relieving himself of a pig he has swallowed, the tail alone remaining in his mouth. Then follow a young man and woman, gaily attired, emblematic of luxury. So far, three of the "sept péchés capitaux" are represented; but after these comes a national subject: a man playing on the bagpipe. The figures throughout the rood-screen are all boldly executed, and the tracery most elegant and delicate.

The painted glass in the church is considerable, and represents the Life of Our Saviour, that of St. Fiacre, the Feast of Herod, and the Martyrdom of the Baptist, figures of the Prophets of the Old Testament, with many others. In most of the subjects, the figures are much mutilated. On one window is inscribed, "Pierre Androuet ouvrier demeurant à Kemperlé 1552." Over one altar is a sculpture, representing the Martyrdom of Saint Sebastian, between two archers, in the quaint costume of the sixteenth century.

About six miles from Le Faouët, is the ruined castle of Poncallec, with its forest, étang, and forge; once the demesne of the young marquis of that name, who was implicated in that conspiracy to transfer the Regency from the Duke of Orleans to Philip V. of Spain, called the plot of Cellamare. Of the hundred and forty-eight gentlemen included in the accusation, all escaped to Spain, except Poncallec and three others. Poncallec refused to accompany them from a superstitious fear, a fortune-teller having foretold he should perish by the sea, "par la mer." They took refuge in a church, but were surprised by a party of cavaliers who had muffled the feet of their horses to reach them unheard. They escaped through a subterranean passage, and, for fifteen days, lay concealed in the hollow of a yew-tree, fed in secret by faithful peasants. Poncallec traversed France in the disguise of a priest, but was arrested at the Pyrenees. He with the three others were all convicted of high treason, and, a few hours after their condemnation, were beheaded at Nantes. Poncallec was the last to suffer. When ascending the scaffold, he asked the executioner his name; on his answering "La Mer," Poncallec felt the witch's prophecy was fulfilled.

The estates of the four victims were confiscated, their arms effaced from the fronts of their houses, the moats of their castles filled in, and their trees (hautes futaies) cut down, "à hauteur d'infamie," that is, within nine feet of the ground, in like manner as were those of Moor Park, after the execution of the Duke of Monmouth. A list was presented to the Regent Philip of other offenders, but he tore the paper, and published an amnesty The story of Poncallec is dramatically told by Alexandre Dumas, in his novel, called 'Une fille du Regent.' The Bretons honoured the victims as martyrs, and M. de la Villemarqué, in his 'Chansons Bretons,' gives a touching elegy which shows the sympathy excited by the tragic fate of Poncallec:

"Quand il arriva à Nantes, il fut jugé et condamné,
 Condamné non par ses pairs,
Mais par des gens tombés de derrière les carrosses.
 Ils demandèrent à Poncallec :
 'Seigneur marquis, qu' avez vous fait ?
 —Mon devoir ; faites notre métier.'
Il est mort, chers pauvres, celui qui vous nourissait,
Qui vous vêtissait, qui vous soutenait ;
Il est mort celui qui vous aimait, habitants de Berné
Celui qui aimait son pays et qui l'a aimé jusqu'à mourir.
 Il est mort à vingt-deux ans
 Comme meurent les martyrs et les saints ;
 Que dieu ait pitié de son âme !
Le seigneur est mort . . . Ma voix s'éteint, . . .
Toi qui l'as trahi, sois maudit, sois maudit ;
 Toi qui l'as trahi, sois maudit."

We left Le Faouët and its comfortable primitive inn, the "Lion d'Or," with much regret; the country around is beautiful, and we had arranged to set out early that we might cross the Montagnes Noires by daylight; but we were disappointed in procuring a carriage, and it was not till late in the afternoon that we were able to leave in a diligence, of which the coupé alone was reserved to us, the interior being occupied by Breton farmers, returning from a horse-fair. From the elevated wooded ground of Le Faouët, the road makes a precipitous descent, and crosses the little stream of Moulin-au-duc, after which it again rises, in a winding direction, along the side of a mountain with a valley and little stream beneath. Then a rapid descent brought us to Gourin, where we would gladly have risked staying the night, and waited till morning to pursue our road over the mountains, but we had paid our fare to Carhaix. Up hill and down again, like all the roads in mountainous Finistère, from Gourin we ascended again and passed a crest of the Montagnes Noires, which separates the three departments of Finistère, Morbihan, and Côtes-du-Nord; and proceeded through a valley to Carhaix, where we arrived at midnight, and therefore had no opportunity of seeing the beauties of the mountain scenery.

Carhaix is a dirty, unpaved, dull town of the middle ages, much decayed from its ancient importance when capital of the country dismembered from Cornouaille, in the sixth century, by Comorre the Breton Bluebeard. It is situated on an eminence, commanding an extensive view of the barren monotonous surrounding country, bounded by the Arré mountains, the Alps of Finistère. It is the centre of Lower Brittany, and the Duke d'Aiguillon, Minister of Louis XV., caused six roads to be made from it to Brest, Quimper, Morlaix, St. Brieux, Vannes, and Châteaulin, with the hope of introducing commerce and civilisation into this barren district, "le dernier trou du monde," as it is styled by the Parisian.

La Tour d'Auvergne, Premier Grenadier de

France, was born here, and a bronze statue of him, by Marochetti, has been erected to his memory. He is in the uniform of a private soldier, and presses to his heart the sword of honour just presented to him by the First Consul. Round the pedestal are four bas-reliefs, representing scenes in his life. In the first, he saves a wounded soldier; in the second, he forces the gates of Chambery; in the third, he takes leave of the parents of a youth, for whom he goes as a substitute into the army. The last represents his death; he was killed by a lance at Ober-hausen (Bavaria), fighting against the Austrians. The monument bears this inscription on its four sides:—

"La Tour d'Auvergne, 1er Grenadier de France, né à Carhaix le 23 Decembre, 1715; mort au champ d'honneur le 27 Juin, 1800.

"Ecrivain, Citoyen, Soldat, sa vie toujours glorieusement remplie ne laisse que de sublimes exemples à la posterité.

"Tant de talens, et de vertus, appartenaient à l'histoire et au premier Consul, de les devancer.

"Celui qui meurt dans une lutte sacrée trouve pour le repos une patrie même sur la terre etrangère."

Preferring the title of "Premier Grenadier de France" to higher honours, La Tour d'Auvergne remained as a private soldier to his death; but in a decree of Buonaparte, then First Consul, preserved in the Musée des Archives, he orders that La Tour d'Auvergne's name should still be kept on the muster-roll of his old regiment; and, when called, the corporal should answer, "Mort au champ d'honneur!"

The moderation and absence of ambition in the character of La Tour d'Auvergne is expressed in a letter to Le Coq, Bishop of Ille-et-Vilaine. He writes,—"Je me prosterne bien plus volontiers devant la Providence pour le remercier que pour rien demander; du pain, du lait, la liberté; et une cœur qui ne puisse jamais s'ouvrir à l'ambition, voilà l'objet de tous mes désirs."

La Tour d'Auvergne had a learned dog, which he educated as a soldier; he went through the whole drill, and his master made him always wear boots. He marched in them, on one occasion, the whole distance from Paris to Guingamp.

A horse fair and market were going on at Carhaix. Some of the women wore curious flannel hoods, edged with colours. There were baskets of burnt limpet shells and lime, used in washing as substitutes for soap. In the porch of the church dedicated to St. Tremeur (son of the Bluebeard Comorre) are some of the little skull-boxes so common in the north of Brittany. One was labelled, "Ci gît le chef de Mr. Thomas François Nonet, ancien notaire et maire de la ville de Carhaix le 28 J^{ier} 1776, décédée le 8 7bre 1842." The curfew bell rings at Carhaix at a quarter to ten.

We left next day for Huelgoat, fifteen miles distant, the road up and down, wild and dreary. At Pont Pierre, about nine miles from Carhaix, we crossed the Aulne, even here a considerable river, with a beautiful thick forest on our right. At a place called La Grande Halte, we turned off the road to the right for Huelgoat, about a mile and a half off. It is prettily situated on a large pond or lake, nearly a mile and a half in circumference, and of great depth (20 feet). It was market day; the men wore brown serge coats, close white breeches and black gaiters, with straw hats bound with black. The countrymen from Saint Herbot were there in their black shaggy goat or sheepskin overcoats, the hair turned outwards (there are flocks of black sheep throughout Finistère), without sleeves, and the white breeches, black gaiters, and straw hats. The women of Huelgoat wear large white turnover collars and caps with long ends turned up.

We first walked to the rocking stone on the slope of a steep hill, considered the third largest in Brittany; the block forming a kind of double cube, that is, about twice the length of its height. It requires a very slight impulse to make it rock. This "fairy stone" is often consulted by the peasants. In the ravine close by, below the path, is what is called the "Cuisine de Madame Marie," but termed in the guide-books the "Ménage de la Vierge;" a recess formed of large masses of fantastically shaped granite rocks, through which a small stream of water flows, arriving thither from the pond, by a subterranean course. One stone, hollowed out, is called the écuelle of the Virgin, and others have each the name of some different utensil requisite for the "Ménage" of our Lady. The young people managed to scramble to the bottom.

Huelgoat (Breton, "high wood") is celebrated for its lead-mines, which are now no longer worked. A well-kept path, cut on the top of the ridge, leads to the mines, about two miles and a half distant, along a neat little canal, three feet wide, issuing from the great pond, and supplying the hydraulic machine used to pump the water out of the mine. The deeply wooded valley, along the ridge of which it runs, is traversed by a rushing stream, which runs over rocks; and at a place called Le Gouffre, the rounded granite masses are piled in the wildest confusion, like those of the Ménage de la Vierge, forming a large dark cavern, at the bottom of which the imprisoned river foams and roars, and has forced itself an escape through a gorge at some distance from the place, where it is lost to view. A young girl is said, about a century back, to have fallen down this gulf. Attempting to gather some of the mosses that line the sides of the rocks, she slipped in and perished in the sight of her intended. Her body never reappeared, but our guide assured us that her ghost was seen four years since, and that sighs and groans are to be heard at eve issuing from the fatal chasm.

The pretty little ivy-leaved campanula was growing here in abundance. We visited in succession the "robber's cave," the "Pierre cintré" (a natural archway), and other wonders, and returned much pleased with the infinite variety of fantastic rocks, rushing waters, and hanging woods, which form this charming scene.

The lead-mines of Huelgoat have been worked since the fifteenth century for the silver which the lead-ore (galena) contains.

The right of working these mines and those of Poullaouen was given by Louis XIII. to Jean du Châtelet, Baron of Beausoleil, and his wife. He was at that time General of the Mines in Hungary, and inspector of the French mines. They were accompanied by German miners, but their mysterious researches caused them to be accused of sorcery and magic. Richelieu had them imprisoned in the Bastille, where they both died, victims of the fanaticism of the age, and the works were abandoned till the eighteenth century. They are now no longer in operation, but it is said are about to be re-opened.

Retracing our steps to La Grande Halte, on the Carhaix road, we turned off to the left to see the cascade of St. Herbot. We left our carriage, and walked up a hill covered with underwood, opposite the fall. The cascade is formed by the little river Elez falling through a mountain gorge about 650 feet in in length, filled with granite rocks of every shape and size, the sides overhung with woods of oak. The height of the fall is 230 feet.

There was no water in the cascade. At the best, it must be only a succession of small falls. The river tumbles from rock to rock, forming on some of the ledges pools of water, filled with small trout, some of which were caught by our party.

According to the legend, a giant of the country, wishing to clear the fields of his friend, a Druid, from the rocks that encumbered them, rolled them down the torrent.

We descended the hill to the road where we had left our carriage, and went to the chapel of St. Herbot, a building of the sixteenth century, on the side of a rushing brook. It has a high square tower opening into the church, and a rood-screen of wood beautifully carved in the style of the Renaissance, which forms three sides round the altar. Two angels are represented with cups, the "sainte graal" receiving the blood of Christ. The entrance to the church is up a flight of steps. It has a beautifully sculptured south porch, with statues of the Apostles, and some fine painted-glass windows. One part of the church has the windows with iron bars, as if for defence.

Near the altar is the tomb of the anchorite, St. Herbot; his effigy reposes under a Gothic canopy,

63. Carved Stalls, St. Herbot.

upon a granite sarcophagus, represented in his hermit's gown, the hood thrown back, flowing hair, long beard, his breviary suspended to his girdle, and his pilgrim's staff by his left arm. His feet repose on a recumbent lion. St. Herbot is the great patron of cattle; the three days of the fair and pardon all the bullocks rest; and when an animal is ill, an offering of his hair is made to the saint. We saw a heap of horsehair and cows' tails lying on one of the altars.

Carved Stalls, St. Herbot.

These are annually sold for the profit of the church, and the proceeds amount to a considerable sum. Our guide gravely assured us that on the first of May, day of the Pardon of St. Herbot, the cows " d'elles mêmes" walk three times round the church.

We returned late to Carhaix, and left next day for Guingamp, passing, about two miles out of the town, through the village of St. Catherine on the Hierre, where the church has fleur-de-lisé windows, like that of Penmarch. We here entered the department of the Côtes-du-Nord through Callac, where we changed horses; the country was hilly and wooded. On the left we saw the spire of the church of Notre Dame-de-Grâces, where repose the remains of Charles of Blois; on the right appeared the cathedral towers of Guingamp. At this last place we took the rail to Caulnes-Dinan, and on, by diligence, to Dinan, whence we proposed returning by St. Malo; but, finding the time of the boat's sailing did not suit our arrangements, we returned by Paris and Dieppe to London.

Some Useful Dates in the History of Brittany.

1320. Du Guesclin born.
1338. Marriage of Charles of Blois and Jeanne de Penthièvre. Du Guesclin at the tournament.
1341. Death of John III. Beginning of the War of Succession.
1342. John de Montfort, prisoner in the Louvre, 1345. Escape to England and death.
1346. Siege of Hennebont defended by Jeanne de Flandre.
1347. Charles of Blois taken prisoner at La Roche Derrien.
,, War of the two Jeannes.
1351. Combat of the Thirty.
1356. Charles of Blois liberated.
1359. Siege of Dinan.
1364. Battle of Auray.
1365. Treaty of Guérande.
1370. Du Guesclin, Constable of France.
1375. John IV. flees to England.
1380. He is recalled.
1387. Death of Du Guesclin.
1387. Clisson marries his daughter to Jean de Penthièvre.
1407. Death of Clisson.
1420. Seizure of John V. by the Penthièvres.
1488. Battle of St. Aubin du Cormier.

CHRONOLOGICAL TABLE OF THE DUKES OF BRITTANY.

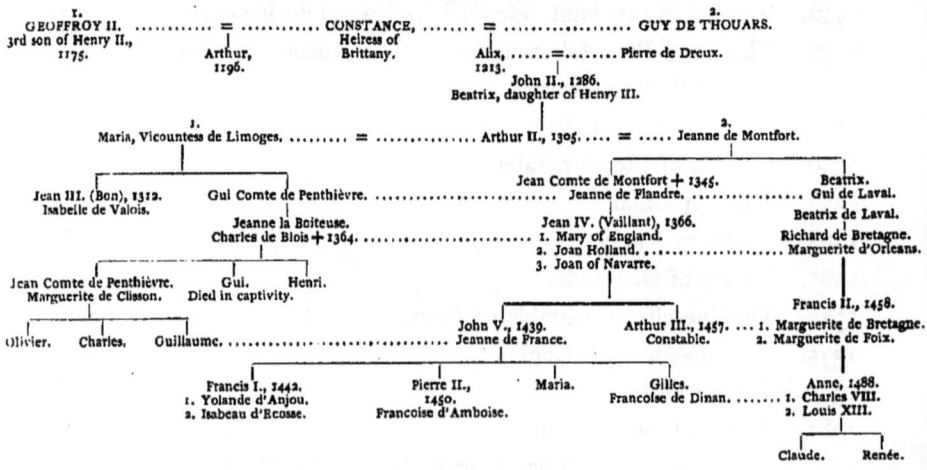

INDEX.

Abelard, 192.
Ancenis, 217.
Angoulême, Duke and Duchess, 167.
Anne, of Austria, Queen, 122, 269.
Anne de Beaujeu, Regent, 203, 229.
Anne of Brittany, Queen-Duchess, 42, 50, 62, 98, 121, 153, 221, 222, 223.
Arré, mountains, 103, 136, 297.
Arthur and Geoffroy Plantagenet, 216.
Arthur III., Duke of Brittany, Constable of France, 190.
Artois, Comte d', 29.
Auray, 157.
Auray, battle of, 161.
Auray, Ste. Anne d', 158.
Avranches, 23.
Audierne, 269.

Baciocchi, Princess, 187.
Baie des Trépassés, 274.
Barbès, 28.
Barkers (aboyeurs), 214.
Bas-Foins, 49.
Beaumanoir Chapel, 56.
Beaumanoir, Jean de, 52, 206.
Beauport, Abbey of, 76.
Belle-Isle-en-Mer, 250.
Bellière, Château of, 54.
Berri, Duchess, 226.
Bertheaume, Island, 128.
Bigouden, 258.
Biniou, 249.
Bisson, 155, 194.
Blanche of Castille, 149.
Blue Beard, Breton, 194.
Boisgelin, Château, 75.
Bonchamps, 237.
Bourg-de-Batz, 217.

Brest, 118.
Bretesch, Château of, 248.
Breton bed, 239; butter, 153; character, 99; chestnuts, 203; cow and pig, 153; distaffs, 259; farmhouse, 86; knitting, 74; soup, 112; threshing, 117; vehicles, 37.

Cancale, 39.
Carnac, 177.
Cesson, Tour de, 71.
Carhaix, 297.
Chalais, Comte de, 226.
Champ des Martyrs, 166.
Champtoceaux, Château de, 218.
Chandos, Sir John, 16, 46, 89, 162.
Châteaubriand, 36, 41.
Châteaulin, 135.
Chatelet, J. du, 302.
Chêne-Ferron, Château of, 57.
Cherbourg, 1.
Charles the Bad, 134.
Charles of Blois, 67, 75, 82, 161.
Charles V., 223.
Charles VI., 185.
Charles VII., 47, 191.
Charles VIII., 203, 229.
Clisson, Constable, 25, 89, 186, 209.
Clisson, Marguerite, 89, 218.
Colomb, Michel, 127, 221.
Combat des Trente, 206.
Combourg, Château de, 36.
Comorre, 194, 297.
Concarneau, 142.
Conquet, Le, 128.
Constance of Brittany, 216.
Cornouaille, 135.
Costume, 23, 133, 140, 234, 249, 258, 283, 288, 298.
Couëron, 34.

Couësnon, 29.
Courcorro, 181.
Coutances, 19.
Crêpes, 11, 169.
Croisic, Le, 232.
Crosses, 104.

D'Andelot, Sieur, 248.
Dinan, 44, 50.
Dinan, Françoise de, *see* Françoise.
Dinan, Roland de, 53.
Dinard, 44.
Dogs of St. Malo, 42.
Dol, 30.
Douarnenez, 276, 279.
Dubourg, 29.
Du Guesclin, 24, 44, 45, 51, 53, 74, 143, 162, 209.

Elven, Château of, 199.
Edward III., 15, 112, 153, 223.
Edward IV., 201.
Escoublac, 232.
Estouteville, Sieur d', 13, 26.
Epinglettes, 160.
Ermine, Order of, 126.

Filet, saint, 264.
Faouët, Le, 287.
Folgoët, Le, 120.
Fouquet, N., 256.
Francis I., Duke of Brittany, 47, 126 *note*, 185.
Francis II., Duke of Brittany, 221, 229.
Françoise de Dinan, 46, 215.
Fontenelle le Ligueur, 267.
Frérie Blanche, 72.
Frobisher, 134.

Gavr' Inis, 174.
Gesril du Papeu, 166, 167.
Gilles de Bretagne, 46.
Goëmon (wrack), 94.
Grallo, King, 139, 275.
Guérande, 245.
Guimiliau, 115.
Granville, 21.
Guingamp, 72.

Hædic, Isle, 250, 257.
Haye du Puits, La, 17.
Harcourt, G. d', 15.
Hennebont, 156.
Henry II., 4, 24, 26.
Henry IV., 71, 134, 191.
Henry V., 13, 26, 134, 201.
Henry VI., 201.
Henry VII., 201.
Henry VIII., 128.
Henri IV., 216, 225.
Hercé, 167, 183.
Hoche, Gen., 166.
Hunaudaye, Château de la, 62.
Huelgoat, 300.

Indian corn, 251.
Inclined axis of church, 106.
Is, City of, 274.
Ingrandes, 217.

James II., 72, 205.
Jean de Montfort, 67, 112, 153.
Jeanne d'Arc, 190.
Jeanne de Flandre (Montfort), 83, 156.
Jeanne de France, 185, 219.
Jeanne de Penthièvre, 83.
Jeanne (Joan) of Navarre, 106, 121, 134, 194, 246.
John I. (Roux), 189, 194.
John II., 204.
John III. (Bon), 67, 160, 205.
John IV. (Victorieux), 25, 67, 71, 119, 121, 126, 160, 185, 223, 246.
John V., 88, 121, 185.
Josselin, Château, 211.
Jugon, 61, 187.

Kergrist, Château, 96.
Kermartin, 84.
Kermario, 177.
Kersanton stone, 122, 135.
Kerserho, 181.
Kerscaven, 269.
Knights Templars. 69.
Knollys, Sir R., 119, 143.
Korn-er-Hoët, 187.

LA FORÊT.

La Forêt, Bay, 143.
La Garaye, Château of, 57.
Lamballe, 67.
Lanleff, 68.
Langoat, 83.
Langoustes, 94, 147.
Lannion, 94.
Lanvaux, Lande de, 187.
Larochejaquelin, 22.
La Tour d'Auvergne, 297.
Lehon Abbey, 56.
Lavandières de la Nuit, 290.
Lesage, 188.
Léonnais, 103.
Léon, Viscounts, 110.
Lézardrieux, 80.
Lessay, 17.
Locmariaker, 170.
Loctudy, 26?.
Lorient, 155.
Louis XI., 26, 201.
Louis XII., 32, 223.
Louis XIV., 119, 189.

Manny, Sir W., 128, 153, 157.
Manoir, 81.
Martinvast, 12.
Matilda, Empress, 3.
Mary, daughter of Edward III., 106.
Mercœur, Duke de, 225.
Menhir, 35.
Mingant Rock, 119.
Minihy (sanctuaries), 88.
Mivoie, Chêne de, 207.
Montafilant, Château, 46.
Montfort, 215.
Mont St. Michel, 25.
Motto of Dukes of Brittany, 126, 161.
Morbihan Sea, 174.
Morlaix, 97.

Nacqueville, Château, 6.
Nantes, 221.
Napoleon I., 3, 4.
Notre Dame-de-Comfort, church, 279.
Notre Dame-du-Roncier, 213.

Octeville, 5.
Ouëssant Isle, 128, 133.

ROSARIES.

Paimbœuf, 229.
Paimpol, 80,
Palais, Le, 251.
Penmarch, 263.
Penmarch, Torche de, 262.
Penthièvre, 149, 210, 225.
Périers, 18.
Perros Guirec, 92.
Peter, Duke, 72.
Philip Augustus, 28.
Pierre de Dreux, 216.
Pierres de Croix, 286.
Pleudaniel, 81.
Ploërmel, 203.
Plouaret, 96.
Plougastel, 133.
Plouharnel, 180.
Ploumanach, 92.
Pointe du Raz, 271.
Pole, W. de la, Earl of Suffolk, 13.
Pontacallec, Marquis de, 226, 294.
Pontaven, 150.
Pontcroix, 276.
Pont l'Abbé, 257.
Pontorson, 24.
Port Navalo, 250.
Potatoes, 251.
Poulignan, 233.
Porzmoguer, 130.

Querqueville, 5.
Quiberon, 165.
Quimper, 138.
Quimperlé, 151.

Rance River, 43.
Richelieu, Cardinal, 96, 119.
Richelieu, Duke, 82.
Rennes, 216.
Retz, Cardinal, 226.
Rieux, Marshal, 202.
River scenery, 103, 216, 250.
Roads, 84, 91.
Roche Bernard, La, 247.
Roche Derrien, La, 82.
Roche Jagu, La, 81.
Rochefort, Chancellor, 229.
Rocking stones, 93, 149, 300.
Rohan family, 98, 99, 111, 210.
Rosaries, 282.

Y

ROSCOFF.

Roscoff, 111.
Rosgrand, 153.
Rosporden, 285.
Rustéphan, Château, 149.

Sacring bells, 279.
Saire, Monk of, 5.
Ste. Anne la Palue, 282.
St. Armal, 204.
— Aubin du Cormier, 229.
Ste. Barbe, 287.
St. Brieuc, 71.
— Corentin, 137.
— Cornély, 178.
— Fiacre, 20.
—   ,,   church, 293.
— Florent, 217.
— Génévroc, 105.
— Germain, 5, 34.
— Gildas, 192.
— Guenolé, 263.
— Herbot, 303.
— Ives, 85, 88.
— Léonard, 75.
— Malo, 39.
— Mathieu, 129.
— Michael, Order of, 26.
— Nazaire, 230.
— Pair, 23.
— Pol de Léon, 103.
— Samson, 32.
— Thégonnec, 114, 117.
— Urlose, 152.
— Vincente Ferrar, 184.
Salt, 233.
Sardine fishery, 144.
Sarzeau, 192.
Scaër, 285.
Scales, Lord, 21.
Sein, Isle, 272.

WILLIAM.

Sevigné, Madame de, 203.
Skull-boxes, 91.
Sœurs de la Miséricorde, 16.
Sœurs de le Providence, 11.
Sombreuil, Comte de, 164, 183, 184.
Stuart, Charles, 113, 230.
Stuart, Mary, 98, 112.
Sucinio, Château, 189.

Teigneuse, Isle, 250.
Thomas à Becket, 24.
Tocqueville, A. de, 7.
Tombeleine, Isle, 28.
Touquédec, Château, 95.
Tourlaville, Château, 7.
Tréguier, 88.
Trégunc, 149.
Trieux River, 80.
Trinité, La, 130.
Tumiac, Butte de, 199.
Typhaine, the Lady, 24, 44, 54.

Valognes, 14.
Vannes, 183.
Varades, 217.
Vendean army, 217.
Veneti, 183.
Venus' ear, 2.
Victoria, Queen, 1, 3, 14.

Walsh, 230.
War of the two Jeannes, 83.
War of Succession, 67 note.
Washing, 18.
Wells, holy, 125, 285.
Welsh Baptists, 100.
William the Conqueror, 4.

THE END.

PRINTED BY WILLIAM CLOWES AND SONS, DUKE STREET, STAMFORD STREET,
AND CHARING CROSS.

www.ingramcontent.com/pod-product-compliance
Lightning Source LLC
Chambersburg PA
CBHW060407170426
43199CB00013B/2032